Joan Cliffo[...]
and broadc[...]
Society of [...]
She is marr[...] [...]o is
Chaplain to the R.A.F. Hospital in Ely.

THANK YOU, PADRE

Memories of
World War II

Edited by
JOAN CLIFFORD

Collins
FOUNT PAPERBACKS

First published in Great Britain by Fount Paperbacks, London
in 1989

Copyright © Joan Clifford 1989

Printed and bound in Great Britain by
William Collins Sons & Co. Ltd, Glasgow

As a young servicewoman in World War II, I accompanied the padre to the church parade and the hymns on the harmonium. It never occurred to me to wonder what he did with the rest of his time. Fifty years later, some of those chaplains still with us have been telling me how they spent those years. Some I approached were too frail to be able to share the past, but most were willing, from the arbitrary list of names I acquired, to dredge up their memories. Sometimes they produced diaries and memoirs at which they had not looked for half a century. For some it was a poignant exercise. For me it was often deeply moving, sometimes enraging, sometimes comical. I made many friends. I salute them.

CONTENTS

ACKNOWLEDGEMENTS

I wish to thank all the former padres who so graciously gave me information and talked to me about their wartime chaplaincies. I am particularly grateful to the ministers and clergy, and relatives of those deceased, who allowed me to read and make use of diaries and memoirs.

I am grateful to the Principals and officers of the three chaplaincy services, and officials of the Ministry of Defence, who made it possible for me to write this book and who were unfailingly courteous and helpful.

I thank Miss Janet Barratt for research, and officials of the British Library, the Imperial War Museum and the Royal Air Force Museum.

Among books consulted, particularly valuable were: *In this Sign Conquer* by Sir John Smyth, V.C. (Mowbray 1968) and *The Sea Chaplains* by the Rev. Gordon Taylor, who graciously allowed me to quote freely from his book.

I am grateful for reading my manuscript and for helpful comments to: Lt.-Col. (Ret'd) R. W. Nye, Departmental Secretary, Royal Army Chaplains' Department Centre; the Reverend Graham T. Corderoy, B.A., formerly Principal Chaplain C.S.F.C., R.A.F.; and the Reverend R. Gwilym Williams, C.B.E., B.A., R.N. (Ret'd).

JOAN CLIFFORD

FOREWORD BY THE ARCHBISHOP OF CANTERBURY

I fought through the closing years of the Second World War as a combatant rather than as a padre. I was not at that time ordained. However, I recognize at once in these valuable pages the paradox of the experience of war. Whilst it often seemed recklessly wasteful of human life, the resolute and courageous action of so many men, combatants and padres alike, revealed the noblest characteristics in the human soul.

In the words of so many of the padres whom Joan Clifford allows to speak for themselves – a rare enough virtue in a book nowadays – I recognize a common experience for Christians caught up in war. It began to make sense of the Cross. We began to experience how at Calvary pain and suffering was transformed into an outpouring of love.

Again and again in this book we read of the triumph of love over pain and death. The padres were the natural focus for Christian reflection and for signals of hope. Their contribution to the war thus seems much greater than their numbers might warrant.

I warmly commend this book. It is a tribute to that noble army of Second World War padres who have been too often overlooked in comparison with the more famous padres of the First World War. Joan

Clifford has set the record straight and allowed these men to speak for themselves and to express how much their subsequent ministries have been deeply enriched by their war-time service.

✝ Robert Cantuar

How they joined

In the tradition of hundreds of years and countless battles, somewhere in the region of five thousand padres went to war in the three armed services in 1939. Many were "regulars" who fully understood service life but were soon to find themselves in unusual parishes. Some were reservists who were quickly called up. Most were men who offered "for the duration" and for whom it was a totally new experience. Clergy and ministers of the different branches of the Church enrolled as chaplains to the Army, the Navy and the Royal Air Force.

Most were volunteers. A few were encouraged by friends or superiors. In his autobiography, the "parachute padre", J. Fraser McLuskey, M.C., tells how a trusted friend said to him, when he was a young university chaplain – "You might like to feel that you had shared in the burden and heat of the day with your friends . . ."

One man, Gwilym Williams, was "volunteered" by his sister. Meeting the secretary of the appropriate Board, she said, "I hear you'll soon be looking for a new naval padre . . ." "Yes, very soon." "Well, the man you want is my brother . . ." "Oh, tell me about him" ". . . he plays rugger . . ."

"What a qualification", says William today, but adds – "She was not far wrong. The fact that I played rugger enabled me to build bridges between myself and the servicemen . . . absolutely essential for an effective ministry."

While some were senior in years, most of the men were young and, though serious in intent, lively lads. Some were enthusiastic, deeply patriotic, some stolidly resolved. Today many yet with us remember quite clearly why they applied. Ross Hook – not, he says, an introspective man – was recommended by his bishop and went into Marine Commandos "because there was a war on". Ronald Bradwell says, "A chaplain goes where there are people to be served – prison, hospital, gunboats, the lot." Vincent Parkin, joining the Royal Air Force, declares, "The war seemed justifiable and soldiering was inevitable for some. As I was the same age as many in the Forces, it seemed right to be with them."

John F. O. Bown was one of several curates in a very large southern parish. His superior called him and said, "John, you're the only one without any encumbrances – how about it?"

A more detailed explanation is now given by Hywel Evans, a wartime destroyer chaplain in the Royal Naval Volunteer Reserve. He recalls standing on the bridge on a fine September day in 1942, on his first convoy duty – it was in fact to be the last of the dangerous daylight twenty-four hour convoys – and reflecting on his situation.

"I thought, What am I doing here, a young curate in a man o' war in the middle of the ocean about to be shot at, with friends all round shooting at similar young men in ships and planes?"

Hywel had clear childhood memories of "old soldiers" in his terrace at home, who had suffered because of the Great War. This had made a deep impression on him, and at university he had voted in a famous debate that he would not "fight for King and Country".

But he goes on: "Much happened after 1935." He speaks of "Hitlerian voices strident for expansion – compulsory enrolment of youth into quasi-army battalions – large development of flying clubs with suspiciously sophisticated aircraft – soon to appear in 1936 in the Nazi intrusion into the Spanish Civil War – the building of the largest battleships in the world – the rapid expansion of a U-boat fleet – and the clearly expressed nature of Nazi society itself.

"So why was I standing here? Weak as we were still, Britain had called a halt to Nazi aggression over threats to Poland, three years earlier. In that time, young men and women had disappeared from 'my' parish, summoned to war. From the outset I knew that I would go with them. So the time came; not to support or 'bless' war but to continue to be with the children of God in their strange and fearsome situations. So I stood on the bridge assured. In human affairs there is no absolute black or white, but the issue of Nazism against humanity was as near as could be . . . we had to remove this major blockage of the path to freedom, in danger of destroying the whole of Western Europe . . ."

Father John Roche says the idea of a chaplaincy was "suggested by my religious Superior, who thought it would be a good experience for me", while Tommy

Goss, presumably with a chuckle, says he "invited the RAF to have me".

Ronald Martin says he got in "by badgering the Bishop of St Albans when I was a curate in Letchworth". Murray Raw says, "I was having supper with the Archbishop of York when I told him I ought to be serving my generation in the Forces. The Archbishop then spoke to Dr Aubrey, General Secretary of the Baptist Union." Francis Cocks had always had a deep interest in the Royal Air Force since childhood in Felixstowe, when successive chaplains-in-chief had been friends of his father, and he himself had been Company Sergeant-Major in the school Officers' Training Corps (O.T.C.).

Dermot Quinlan says, "I was a curate at St James's in Belfast. In 1940 I realized many young men were serving although there was no conscription in Ireland. They needed to be ministered to so I joined."

Several use the words "cruel and painful necessity". Arthur Jestice says, "I questioned the rightness of the First World War but felt that our war was an inevitable consequence of the first and the mistakes made following it. As things were, something had to be done." Kenneth Holt believed "Men and women serving in the Armed Forces needed religious faith just as much if not more than those not in the Forces." Neville Metcalfe felt "It was a privilege to serve with those who were giving so much. It enabled me to get alongside all ranks in a way not easy to emulate with people in everyday circumstances."

The padres came from varied situations. Some were from curacies where they were expected to have served for at least three years, and where they often had to find their own replacements. Some came directly from theological college. David Izzett volunteered in Ceylon, when the school of which he was headmaster was commandeered as a hospital; Alfred Cook after missionary service in Nigeria; and Stanley Hollis after a previous chaplaincy in India.

These young men had first to submit themselves to the appropriate chaplaincy board and, having been accepted, were then posted to a service unit. In the early days the processes of selection were basic. Harry Lannigan was asked, "Mr Lannigan, do you realize that in the army you will hear a lot of bad language?" To this he replied, "Sir, I come from Glasgow . . ."

Norman Hurst says, "I went up to London for an interview with the Chief Chaplain and he said, 'If you pass the medical, you're in.' It was the easiest interview I've ever had." The "medicals" themselves were sometimes a source of amusement. Raymond Bowers asserts that he was asked if his legs worked all right; this was followed by the enquiry "When you're preaching in the pulpit, can you see the congregation?" On my replying "Yes", he said, "OK. You're A.1." The whole operation took only a few minutes.

"Training" in the early days was also sketchy, though it consolidated in time. Raymond Bowers recalls going to Tidworth on a short course for all denominations, when they had "lectures and a little square-bashing. An awful lot of time was spent in learning how to fill out forms and write memos. We did a little field work and a map-reading exercise, when most of us got lost . . . I can't remember much help offered spiritually or on how to approach our task on the pastoral side, but a good deal of attention was paid to welfare work."

Another man recalls, "Only three things stood out . . . how to fill in a claim for expenses, how to salute, and information that in the field we should be given a three-ton truck fitted out as a mobile chapel, which would double as sleeping quarters. After five years in the service and eighteen in the T.A. (Territorial Army), I am still looking for this truck. I never found it nor anyone else who has.

"Proud in my new uniform, with everything shining, down to my new brown shoes and not forgetting my swagger cane, my pride was soon shattered. Just as I stepped out of the door, two M.P.s were passing. Both looked about ten feet high and threw smart salutes. It was obvious that they could not hide their feelings that I was a very raw recruit indeed. My last 'salute' had been with the Cubs! I knew I had to reply and brought my head down to meet my hand halfway. I was quite relieved that they did not arrest me."

In 1940, when training was still fluid, Ronald Goulding, aged twenty-four, was also conscious of being "without much training or initiation but gloriously attired in officer's uniform and resplendent with Squadron Leader's stripes. I was ushered into RAF Uxbridge – the sort of Buckingham Palace of the Royal Air Force. I saluted the first person wearing a peaked cap, who turned out to be a Warrant Officer. He said, 'Don't worry, sir – they all do it'."

Naval chaplains held no rank. Their initial training – of the temporary chaplains, R.N.V.R. (Royal Naval Volunteer Reserve) – took place at the Royal Naval Barracks at Chatham, Portsmouth and Devonport. In a few weeks they needed to learn something of the traditions, customs, discipline and etiquette of the Royal Navy, and it had to be done quickly.

Young padres were often put under the wing of an experienced Senior Chaplain. Sometimes this worked, and Brynmor Salmon was hopeful when appointed to Portsmouth. He was met by the Senior Chaplain, who took him round the barracks, introduced him to the Company Commander – and then promptly went on leave.

Padres were commissioned as Captains in the Army and as Squadron Leaders in the Royal Air Force.

A first entrance into the mess could be a trial for some young fellows. "It was an awful ordeal", wrote Harry Lannigan. "I realized how little I knew about army mess etiquette. However, the Colonel was friendly and eased things for me considerably." Some continued to find this difficult, and Ronald Goulding admits, "I felt out of my depth mostly in the Officers' Mess, where I had to live in an environment and among people with whom I was entirely unfamiliar." The Commanding Officer could make a great difference. One man speaks of his C.O. as "Very class-conscious".

An ex-naval padre, Max Woodward, remembers learning very quickly the meaning of "the Silent Service". On his first morning in the wardroom he quietly and respectfully said to the Commander, "Good morning, sir". The Commander detached himself from his book and replied crisply, "Bit hearty this morning, aren't you, padre?"

In 1940 some twenty-four R.A.F. chaplains of all denominations were sent to Cranwell for a few days to introduce them to the service. The very correct Station Commander insisted they should march to and from their various activities in two squads. An airman recovering from a rough night out came from the hangar for a smoke and saw twelve padres in full uniform advancing towards him. In horror he rushed through the hangar to the other side and saw twelve more. "Gawd," he cried, "I've had a sinner's nightmare!"

—••‡✗‡••—

Experience quickly taught the padres how to deal with social situations, but different temperaments reacted in different ways to mess life and to service life in general. There would always be those offended by one bawdy joke and for whom service concert parties and mess celebrations would generally prove embarrassing. Many, though, experienced no problems in hard-drinking messes or rough and ready mess-decks.

Some padres were going to feel frustrated. Others, in situations they could hardly have envisaged, would be fully stretched and would discover amazing opportunities. Most found that their faith stood, though before the end of hostilities some would have plumbed the depths of tragedy. But as they were posted and set off for what lay before them, though their pastoral skills were often limited and immature, they took with them strong convictions as to the basic integrity of the Christian faith and a desire to be true to their vocation, whatever branch of the Christian Church they represented.

No women chaplains were appointed during World War II, but a Congregational minister, the Rev. Elsie Chamberlain, became a chaplain after the war – a Squadron Officer at Cranwell. She now says, "They wouldn't fight for a woman chaplain till the war was won!"

However, under the aegis of the Churches' Work for Women in the Forces, twelve woman Chaplains' Assistants were appointed in June 1942, working among members of the Auxiliary Territorial Service (A.T.S.) and the Women's Auxiliary Air Force (W.A.A.F.). They were civilians and provided a link between the "home churches" and the women in uniform.

Some young padres were amazed at the rapid thrust of responsibility upon them, yet they usually coped. Gordon Taylor, now a dignified figure in charge of a famous old London church, was already, at twenty-eight, a man of four years' experience and one hundred thousand miles of seafaring behind him. He had already served in North Atlantic destroyers and South Atlantic armed merchant cruisers, when to his surprise he was appointed chaplain of the battleship *HMS Rodney*, then working off the Normandy beaches as part of the bombardment squadron. These ships were subsequently called by Naval Historian John Winton the "last of the dinosaurs". Says Gordon, "The *Rodney* was a vast iron city – 40,000 tons – with some of the heaviest naval guns in the world."

Today he muses on the "awesome responsibility" he felt, for he was the sole chaplain on board a ship with a complement of more than fifteen hundred officers and men. "When I was taken into the wardroom to meet the Officers, some clearly regarded me as extremely young for my task. But when I told them the *Rodney* was my fifth seagoing ship since 1941, their concern was somewhat allayed . . ."

What they did

The duties of a padre could be summed up as "religious and welfare" – a true but inadequate description. One said, "Oh, we simply carried on with our normal job but in different circumstances". This seems bare. Not many clergy or ministers would presumably be accustomed to the large congregations of many compulsory church parade services, or to facing such lively, uninhibited young men and women, the majority probably reluctant attenders. As one padre wrote: "I felt I was one of the generation, about the first to grow up in the world, in which to be one of those who regularly worship is to be exceptional."

Some padres found themselves involved in duties for which they would have said they were not trained at their theological colleges. Ronald Goulding was sent to Morecambe where there were three thousand W.A.A.F. and admits to "feeling out of my depth".

However, first and foremost, they strove to maintain the celebration of traditional church services, according to their denominations, in days of limited ecumenical vision and practice. They preached sermons, offered prayers and celebrated Holy Communion or said Mass. All insist that the fluidity of troop movements was their greatest practical problem. "I arranged one night to say Mass in the morning – but when I arrived early – everybody had disappeared."

When things were quiet, there were usually few organizational problems, though Tommy Goss recalls that "At Gravesend, the facilities on this cramped one-squadron night-fighter station were minimal."

While in England, padres would carry out normal duties, marrying and christening and preparing people for confirmation. Overseas, it was a question of "being with the men and witnessing for Christ by friendship and sympathy rather than by preaching", says Gordon Brigg. Many former padres stress the identification they strove to make with the men to whom they ministered – according to Jamie Mack, "Being with the men in all situations, doing as they did as far as possible, without carrying arms." Thus David Izzett says, "I was a regimental chaplain – with the Gunners in the jungle, with Signals in Egypt, and as a garrison chaplain in Jerusalem . . ."

Some did an immense amount of travelling. An ack-ack (anti-aircraft) padre could probably travel up to seventy miles a day to visit his flock. One R.A.F. padre visited radio units all over the Shetlands as far north as Unst.

Free Church padre Ronald Bradwell, ex-Navy, speaks ruefully of "the total inadequacy of the numbers of chaplains. One Catholic and one Church of Scotland and Free Church for the whole of Sicily, the Adriatic coast of Italy, Yugoslavia and the Islands, for shore bases and ships in harbour. I seemed to be on the go all the time."

Murray Raw, Air Force padre, remembers, "In the forward area of India, I agreed to care for Protestants in the observer units. There were two dozen of these, deployed in a line from Chittagong to Assam. Each was manned by three wireless operators and three general duties men commanded by a corporal. The first stage was by boat, the second by dugout canoe. Then I walked. First stage here, a climb of four thousand feet to the capital of South Lushai, now known as Mizo. During another stage I climbed to a unit five thousand feet up. At each post I held a service round the dining-room table, followed by discussion. Usually I was welcome. In all, in six weeks, I walked one hundred and eighty miles . . ."

Some were much aware of the plight of lonely units and stations. "In North Africa", says Arthur Jestice, "I tried to visit the small isolated radar stations." Herbert Davies, before being captured in Hong Kong, visited his flock in the outlying pillboxes. "I knew every man's name and every man's family by their photographs, and before I left, I used to say, 'Let's have a few prayers . . .'"

Destroyers, the "maids of all work", usually bore one chaplain for each flotilla, and the padre was expected to move from one to another of the ships, a roving parish. "It was a job", says Gordon Taylor, "for the young and reckless, and meant living in a suitcase."

He remembers the time he served in the *Arrow* in 1941. "The shriek of the wind in the shrouds, the unceasing ping of the searching Asdic, the drenching spray as the ship thudded into each oncoming wave and then rose upon it, the loneliness amid all the dull green or grey-black expanse of the ocean all round, and the occasional appearance of the long black shape of a shadowing German Focke-Wulf 'Kondor' bomber.

It took time to get your sea-legs, upset at first by the smell of oil and of cooking from the galley."

Nevertheless, the excitement of such constant seafaring was a great thrill to a young chaplain. Gordon recalls the successful drill he adopted, of visiting the mess-decks every evening after dinner. "Within an hour of joining my ship I visited the seamen's and the stokers' mess-decks – it was important to establish a reputation for giving equal attention to officers and men. Then, when they wanted to talk to me, we had already met."

As the war proceeded, new ideas were thought up. Padres' Hours were instituted by the Army which, according to Jamie Mack, became "debates where one had to take on anything and everything". Moral Leadership courses were initiated and rapidly accepted by the Air Ministry, and were put on an official basis. They were adopted by all denominations, including Jewish servicemen.

"I myself", says Francis Cocks, "spoke on these courses in Rome, Hamburg, Indian hill stations and an island off Singapore. All kinds of ideas were chewed over and a great deal of muddled theological and ethical thinking straightened out."

——•‡ ✕ ‡•——

Many padres at some time found themselves assisting medical staff, as well as visiting the sick and wounded. There was much to learn – even a stretcher might not be the simple object it seemed, as Harry Lannigan found on going out to collect a wounded man. "One difficulty with a stretcher is that if you carry it open and flat you could be carrying a weapon; if it is rolled up, it could be concealing a weapon . . ."

They had to come to terms with the sight of wounded men. Gradually they assimilated the feeling of the men alongside them for their wounded comrades. A padre with the Infantry in Sicily found "men could put up with being covered in blood from a wounded man, but the moment he died, his blood made them vomit". Also, he could not take cigarettes from a dead man and hand them straight round. "You had to put them first into your own cigarette case, and though the men knew perfectly well where they came from, only then would they accept them."

The padre often came into his own in the dressing station, and here he ministered, writing letters, kneeling beside beds and stretchers, lighting cigarettes, saying prayers with those who asked for this, and gripping many a hand.

W. Vine Russell remembers a special duty that gave him satisfaction relating to the time after the Normandy landings, when wounded were brought home on tank-landing craft. Along with these came the walking wounded who were "bomb happy" after various nasty experiences, such as being bombed over hedges and in ditches, badly affecting their brains, ears and hands, which shook as though with Parkinson's disease.

"These chaps", says Russell, "were accommodated quietly and separately to try to recuperate and rehabilitate. They needed special attention. They always wanted to do things with their hands to prove they could – often things they had never done before, like putting old watches together. They showed a quite pathetic appreciation of any improvement. I felt it was my duty to help here, when I saw this need."

"Welfare" included much letter-writing on behalf of personnel, and sometimes censoring letters people wrote home. This could often cause a smile. Some men wrote to girl-friends exactly as taught to write letters at school. Others wrote exactly as they spoke — every third word being "effing". One young man wrote passionate letters to over forty girls nearly every week. One padre recalls that he himself once broke secrecy by sending his mother a small piece of lace. "Probably no British censor or German agent would have understood, but my mother knew at once that it was Cyprus lace."

Entertainment and sport were often in the hands of padres. Francis Cocks reminds us that "R.A.F. stations being static, and until 1944 largely confined to this country, to some extent the old peacetime routines continued. Even on operational stations, there was plenty of sport. Because of my own athletic background, I found myself at Cranwell in charge of cricket and rugby."

Cinema shows and concerts had to be organized. The latter were sometimes endurance tests for padres and occasionally the cause of embarrassment. Tommy Goss confesses "theatricals of all sorts were my main hobby" and obviously enjoyed this activity, whereas Stanley Betts, in his nine-year chaplaincy, "advised chaplains not to be entertainment officers, since I had the experience of being held responsible for a performance in bad taste".

This was sometimes difficult to avoid. Bill Story recalls being summoned by O.C. Troops in Cyprus to clean up the island concert party, the "Browned-Offs". "At the next performance, I had to go backstage at the crucial moment when the comic started. Later, I was called in again by the O.C. – the Matron had complained. I sent for the comic and told him he must stick to his script."

On a troopship from Egypt to Burma, Neville Metcalfe remembers his time as entertainments officer. "Apart from organizing whist drives and sporting events, I was prevailed on to arrange a boxing competition and also to enter as a contestant . . . as a result the chaplain gained a black eye, an added attraction for the lads to attend my religious service on deck!"

Special gifts often led to special duties. When Father Joe Gill, S.J., went for his medical he was noted as being "the one who speaks Greek". It was tacitly agreed that he should go to Greece and he was soon on his way to Athens. His knowledge of the language served others well in Greece and later in Crete.

Brynmor Salmon found that welfare work seemed to dominate his chaplaincy, and feels he had been prepared for this by his previous ministry in the dockside area of the Manchester Ship Canal. Some jobs sprang out of need, and many padres began to organize library and record facilities. W. Vine Russell was seconded to the BBC for Forces and Pacific Network as Religious Organizer of Forces programmes.

"We prepared a daily service and Sunday Half-hour. The response was good, especially to Programme

Cinderella, made especially for isolated units – gun sites, searchlight batteries, etc. We even had appreciative letters from the Azores."

Among unusual appointments was one for a naval chaplain to go to the isolated island of Tristan da Cunha, almost halfway between South Africa and South America. A secret meteorological station was set up there, and quietly a doctor and a chaplain landed. The chaplain, Cyril Lawrence, gave valuable service to the islanders and possessed an amazing range of abilities. He taught, built, planted, and was an expert in navigation and seamanship, which knowledge he passed on to the boys of the island.

Interviews and counselling occupied the padres. These were often domestic in content. Many men, after being away for about two years, began to worry about the faithfulness of their wives. Matrimonial problems were legion. A man who had been separated from his wife by war for over five years was certainly surprised to receive a telegram stating: "Darling, you are now the proud father of a son . . ."

One padre recalls a colleague, a rather dour Scottish naval chaplain, towards the end of hostilities, when a young rating came to ask for support for Home Compassionate Leave. Asked the reason, he explained that his wife was having yet another baby. The Scottish padre exploded. "It isn't compassionate leave you require, laddie – it's confining to barracks . . ."

Yet another lad had decided he must exchange his wife for the barmaid at the local pub – a glorious colleen – and was in something of a state. The padre says, "I had to fix him. I pulled strings and sent him home on a weekend's leave, he promising me – by all the saints — that he would make a clean breast of things to his wife. Then I persuaded the Training Commander to send an urgent telegram on Sunday to be delivered by a military policeman recalling him back to duty ... to a ship about to sail away on a rather long voyage. As St Paul once said, we are to flee temptation if we cannot fight it. I just helped to speed him on his way . . ."

Sombre moments centred on the deaths of service personnel. It was often the chaplain's task to write to bereaved relatives or to go and report to them. The test pilot who flew an early Halifax, though an ace pilot, did not know the plane and it defeated him. The padre was rung up to break the news to the Flight Sergeant's wife. He hurried down the street. The young woman came down the stairs singing.

"O God," thought the padre, "I have news for you that will take the song out of your mouth." He now says, "I have broken the news of the deaths of so many R.A.F. men but somehow this one affected me very deeply . . . a few nights later my wife and I were sitting behind a friend and his wife at the cinema . . . the next day I had to break the news to her . . ."

Inevitably, along with the letters and visits came the funerals, and these could be on a massive scale. Ronald Bradwell remembers an ammunition ship blowing up in Bari harbour on the Adriatic coast, towards the end of the Italian campaign. Hundreds of Italians were killed and some two hundred Allied Army, Navy and Air Force personnel. The Catholic naval chaplain and chaplain Bradwell went to the port to try to help with the identification of naval ratings and officers. "It was a gruesome task. I shall never forget the sight and sound of a Scots regiment pipe band coming in playing a lament – 'Over the sea to Skye' I think . . . denominational barriers were meaningless that day."

Some padres, looking back, tend to dismiss their activities as "Just pastoral – nothing very exciting". Yet their duties were valuable. One who worked valiantly on shore was Owen Ralph Fulljames, who had joined the naval chaplaincy service originally in 1929. After leaving, he was mobilized in 1937. In 1939 he began three years at the R.N. base in Liverpool. He now recalls, "Life was a mixture – sorrow – counselling by listening – meeting every destroyer or corvette as they came in from their convoy, with their mail, whatever the time of day or night. I took services on Sundays. I visited the sick and wounded who would be put ashore in any of six hospitals. I visited those under punishment, in the common prison. I cadged money from any source to provide fresh vegetables, fruit, sweets – I got to know the leading companies, people, theatres, cinemas, so that men on short leave could be entertained.

"I called on working parties, to cadge woollens, clothing for survivors. This may sound a muddle, but unlike Devonport, Portsmouth or Chatham, where all these amenities existed in barracks, messes, hospitals, the war had moved its theatre to Liverpool, from which the Battle of the Atlantic was eventually fought. The Dean of the Cathedral became the friend of all.

"People like Sir Malcolm Sargent and Dame Sybil Thorndike would come to Gladstone Dock to entertain or have a drink on board to help those who came back from convoy. These men were sometimes shattered beyond endurance by what they had undergone – in watching others getting blown up, ships sink, men covered in oil – the losses at sea, then getting worse, and all the time people asking 'When is the war going to start?'"

After he left this post to plough the Arctic Circle, Owen Fulljames received a service book for the ship's chapel inscribed:

Given by the Dean and Chapter of Liverpool
Cathedral
to the Rev. O. R. Fulljames chaplain R.N.
in gratitude for his great work
in the Port of Liverpool 1939–1942.

This book was returned to Mr Fulljames by order of the Admiralty when the ship was finally paid off.

"I just wondered," says Fulljames, "what I had done in Liverpool."

—•◦•—

3

Relationships

Padres should be able to get on well with people. They not only need to mix socially but also to stand in their priestly relationships. There seem to be few rules about how to achieve this, and some chaplains, in war as in peace, are more successful than others.

Some padres of World War II were already experienced chaplains, others were carried along at first by youth and keenness and, some indicate, by an aptitude for sport, which quickly broke down barriers. Others, of more introvert nature, needed time to cut through the familiar stereotyping.

As has been said, the padres of the Army and Royal Air Force carried rank, those of the Navy did not. There are various views on this. Ross Hook, formerly of the Navy, believes the lack of commissioned rank made person-to-person relationships easier. The Chaplain of the Fleet had said, "You take the rank of the man you're talking to – today you may be an Admiral – tomorrow, a stoker . . ." Gwilym Williams adds, "The clerical collar is the naval padre's badge. He is inferior to none; superior to none. He is one of the ship's company and belongs."

On the other hand, Robert Clements, ex-R.A.F., thinks "the relative rank did help". G. C. Harding thinks "rank was a barrier but one could get past it by being oneself". Francis Cocks, also ex-R.A.F., comments "Officer status is sometimes advanced as a hindrance to relationships, but I believe that given the service structure it need not be so, provided the padre is conscious that he is first and foremost a padre. My American counterparts were always complimentary on the fact that we wore dog-collars."

Father Pat Rorke puts it in these simple words: "The fact of the priesthood transcends all ranks."

Francis Cocks goes on to talk about the relationship between the padre and his Commanding Officer. "I do not remember ever being treated badly, though some Commanding Officers were more sympathetic to one's role than others. My only rough encounter came with a C.O. who clearly did not like chaplains at all."

This is echoed by a padre who received the greeting, "I have no time for bloody padres". Another finds he wrote in his wartime diary, after a wearying journey alone to India, "No sort of welcome – not even a handshake – no attempt to find out what I needed – anxious to pass the baby. A complete indifference to responsibility towards a new chaplain."

These seem to have been rare occurrences. While some speak of C.O.s who were "suspicious of parsons on principle", most agree that relationships were easy and that they had no complaints. One murmurs that "some of the blue-blooded regular Army types took months to recognize your presence". Another feels that "Some service high-ups regarded the padre as part of the establishment and expected support in all disciplinary decisions."

But Father Joe Gill says, "I always met with courtesy and co-operation; I never had any difficulties in any units in getting information about services published in Orders, or in obtaining a reasonable location, or the co-operation of Adjutants and Commanding Officers and Transport Officers."

Some Commanding Officers actively sought a padre. W. H. Miller, chaplain to the famous Chindits, wrote that "Wingate asked for C. of E. chaplains to go with them and to train with the men, and required them to do the same work as the men – ride, march, etc., and to be under thirty-five and fit! . . . We got tired and hungry but Wingate did not spare us; there was physical strain, nervous tension, the huge weight of the equipment." He reported that at first he felt slightly disillusioned and had little opportunity for his distinctive work, but the C.O. said, "Don't worry; think of yourself as part of the family; without the padre the family is incomplete. Your turn will come." It did!

Fifty years ago, ecumenism was less advanced, and some problems arose between different branches of the Church, with non-Anglicans feeling at times disadvantaged. An ex-padre with long experience as a chaplain points out that denominations mattered a great deal in garrisons, stations and shore establishments, but that everything was different on active service. As the war stretched on, denominational barriers seemed to matter less and less. Wrote Harry Lannigan in his diary, during the Battle of Sangro, "By this time my war experiences have completely shattered all denominational thinking in me. The war has revealed to me the stupidity of our divisions."

Once integrated, padres seemed well able to get alongside the members of the Officers' Mess. D. W. Quinlan, twenty-two years a chaplain, says, "As in other walks of life, one tends to relate more easily to people who share common interests. Officers were easier because we shared a common concern for the men."

With regard to N.C.O.s and Other Ranks, most padres report receiving "courtesy and co-operation", though they insist that to gain friendship and genuine respect they had to earn it. One says that the old advice to "Look after those in the guard room and the sick bay" still holds good. All accepted that they were known as "Sky pilots", "God-botherers", "Devil Dodgers", "Bible punchers", etc., but usually in a friendly way.

It was essential to break through the usual stereotyping. Raymond Bowers, chaplain to the 10th Battalion Parachute Regiment, gives an example. In his early days, he went on a training course on firing ranges in Yorkshire. "It was terrible weather. I got a sleeping bag and in total darkness and pouring rain, started the ascent back to the fox holes. Incredibly weary, I let go of the chap in front, slithered and fell into a shell hole. I stumbled out and caught up. I climbed exhausted into my sleeping bag and was nearly asleep when I heard two lads talking. 'Who was that silly . . . who fell into the shell hole?' Other chap – 'Oh, I think it must have been the padre, 'cos he didn't say anything . . .'"

Neville Metcalfe stressed that he "endeavoured to maintain a balance by spending time not only in the Officers' Mess but also in the Sergeants' Mess and the Soldiers' Mess tents." Before being in action with formations, relationships were somewhat formal, but during and after action, friendship and understanding blossomed amazingly.

"I went out of my way", he says, "to show that I had a deep interest in individuals' backgrounds. I found that conversations about homes and backgrounds usually brought me into their confidence."

Not surprisingly, "old sweats" in all three services sometimes proved a trial to young and inexperienced padres but had to be faced. "On the whole," says A. E. Cook, "we were looked on as friends at court and were the subject of much teasing but also recipients of many confidences." Jamie Mack, with the Parachute Regiment, says, "After one was accepted, I felt I was regarded as one of the team and treated generously – at any suggestion of danger, they made it clear they would guard the padre – and they did."

The batman/driver was a key figure. An old book from the first war reminds us that "a wise padre does not look out for a good young man of ecclesiastical turn of mind, but chooses an old soldier for his servant. Such has his feelings and it is not always sensible to ask him where things come from." So, in the last war, one former padre remembers his driver/batman who had been "released" from the Colonel's service. The reason soon became clear. The man was "a terrible driver" but was also "a fine chap and a wonderful scrounger".

Eric Alsop, who served with the Desert Air Force near Tobruk, is not likely ever to forget his "L.A.C. Fred", in civilian life an East End booth-fighter and a debt collector. Says Alsop, "One day an airman said something about me to which Fred took exception. So he hit him one and knocked him out . . . this led to trouble. I got Fred off a charge and urged him not again on my behalf to resort to brute force. But he was a great chap, loyal to the service and to his church. I suppose nowadays he would be called my 'Minder'. He was a marvel too with the wheezy harmonium. And he knew the dihedral of enemy aircraft as well as the back streets of London's East End. 'Run for it, padre!' he would yell."

A Senior Naval Padre gave good advice to newcomers to the Senior Service: "Never discuss affairs of ratings or ship's company in the Wardroom. Especially when censoring letters. Avoid anything that may label you as an 'Officers' person' — like always playing bridge with the same section — be accessible — get to know Divisional Officers — they can keep you in touch as regards welfare. Never betray a confidence or carry tales to the Wardroom. A chaplain can easily be thought of as a spy — sailors, like elephants, never forget!" He also added a word about "sensible drinking", echoed by other former padres. His final word — "keep sermons short".

Stanley Hollis, R.A.F., remembers "The comradeship of crews, members of a Squadron . . . I saw them off from the end of the runway and welcomed them back when they returned. The last view of a plane taking off was 'Tail-end Charlie' with his thumbs up. Of course some did not return in the early hours. Some padres found restraints with aircrews, whom they found 'hard' — but understandably, since they lived under enormous pressure. Some thought things would have been better if the padres had been allowed to fly on missions with them. This was arguable."

One padre who had passed out earlier at Cranwell as a Warrant Officer (W/O) Air Gunner, was asked by the C.O. if he would fly with his Squadron. "I'd be grateful if you would, because conditions here are very tough indeed." This same padre, as he walked into the mess, was greeted by a young officer: "A . . . padre! We've never seen one before! And he's wearing an Air Gunner's brevet! Come and meet the boys." A Flight Lieutenant immediately asked, "Would you like to fly with me tomorrow? We're doing a low level." The following day the padre was airborne and very impressed indeed with the boys.

Life on troopships was an education for young chaplains. Harry Lannigan was interested in hearing servicemen's preferences. "Those who sailed in the Merchant Navy could not understand how anybody could want to be a soldier and run all those risks, while the soldiers would express themselves strongly at having nothing but water under foot."

Bill Story recalls the P. and O. *Strathmore* — "a splendid ship carrying three thousand troops, five hundred officers and two hundred nursing sisters; I was the only chaplain on board. Every night after dinner my cabin was filled with young people eager to talk about life, death, religion, morals, philosophy — till two in the morning. It was fascinating but exhausting."

When Harry Lannigan landed he found himself most at home in the Sergeants' Mess. "I would have trusted my life to any one of them and they would have given their life for anyone. There was no trace of hypocrisy. I was in for a shock, though, through my upbringing. To most of these men, nearly all regular soldiers, sex was a necessity. They alleged they were not being unfaithful to their wives, but merely keeping in training. They may have really believed this. I was often invited to 'ask their wives'. I did not take up this invitation."

Women flit through the reminiscences – civilians, nurses, servicewomen, lonely wives. One padre recalls a young nurse who, at a dance, told him she hated the Germans and hoped she would never have one in her care. Two of her brothers had already been killed and the third blinded.

"One day I went to the tent and found Mary on her knees with her arms round a young German soldier who was badly wounded. She was comforting him. When she saw me she rose, embarrassed. I said quietly 'I wish we could all hate like this'. With a stiff upper lip she replied, 'I am only doing my job – I am a nurse'."

Relations with the enemy were naturally variable according to circumstances. Many padres speak of the German soldiers as "correct" in behaviour, and one recalls a badly-burned British airman describing the tender nursing of a German nun. Early in the war, a padre encountered a "friendly German Christian" in a Dutch hospital. This fellow invited the padre to visit him when the war was over and wrote his name and address in the padre's Army prayer book. "The Gestapo were soon on to this and I was aggressively questioned. I finally made a statement. I wondered what happened to that man who had been a member of a Panzer division."

Vivid little flashes of memory occur. A former Royal Naval chaplain recalls at the end of the war watching

the comings and goings of surrendered German officers who had to come aboard to tell the Royal Navy
the whereabouts of German minefields in the North
Sea. There was some debate as to whether they should
be saluted as they came up the ladder. "I recall the
Chief Bosun's Mate, a Chief Petty Officer, who had
been required to 'pipe' them aboard, afterwards
throwing his silver 'call' into the water in disgust . . ."

Relations between our own troops and Allied troops
could be volatile. Sometimes they were very good.
Geoffrey Harding remembers the time he spent in a
secret camp with the American First Division, the
spearhead of the Normandy invasion. He says, "I
marvelled that so many young men from Nebraska
and Arkansas, Wyoming and Virginia had come so far
across an ocean they had never before seen to risk
their lives in what must have seemed to some to be
someone else's quarrel. We formed the highest opin-
ion of their courage. We got on very well together,
though our idea of humour was so different from
theirs."

Other people encountered in the passing show
included civilians and refugees. All drew a response
from the padres. "I was saddened by the suffering of
the civilian population", one wrote home in the last
days of the war in Italy. "We had fought our way
across yet another river and I made my way where a
Red Cross flag was flying. The village had set up a
hospital in the basement of a church and it was
crowded with wounded men, women and children.
Here was one cost of war, the bewildered and truly
innocent, the ones who had to suffer."

And at the end of the war, the plight of the refugees

was distressing. Bill Story says, "As we got deeper into Austria, the throng grew dense. The sides of the road and railway were built up with shelters of sacking, petrol tins, to keep out wind and rain. Men, women and kids from almost every country in Europe squatted there, waiting for someone to take them home. Crowds filled the roads, pushing loaded prams or barrows, some facing East, some West. It was a tide of human wreckage and misery. Thousands had become stateless."

A comment was made on the danger for an occupying army of "Feeling superior to the conquered people. Even when you thought you were unaffected, it jumped out at you."

With the end of the fighting came orders about fraternization with the enemy, not always easy to carry out. As Bill Story says, "With the Austrians there was a very strict non-frat order. This was difficult to maintain as sex-starved soldiers found beautiful Fräuleins eager to trade all for a tin of Spam."

Harry Lannigan points out that, having insisted on unconditional surrender, we were entirely responsible for feeding the surrounding soldiers, also civilians. Suddenly we were confronted with millions of mouths to feed. "It was heartbreaking. Once I asked the Q.M. (Quarter Master) if I could help and he sent me to take the meat ration to a camp where German girls were being held. He handed me the 'ration' – one horse's head, complete with skin, eyes and teeth. I nearly cried as I handed it over . . ."

Eventually, the padres who had survived the war went home. Some had been away for five or more years. They had their own personal relationships to

remake. Raymond Bowers tells how he excitedly tried
to ring through to his wife and had a job dealing with
the new-fangled telephone. "Her first words, after our
long separation, were 'Press button A, you ass!'" They
were in touch again.

—••**❤︎**••—

Several padres pay tribute to the support of the
various Chaplains' departments. H. Connop-Price says
it was impressive how the department "treated us all
with consideration and courtesy with regard to post-
ings. There was real pastoral concern and support."
Another speaks with affection for his Senior Chaplain,
V. J. Vaughan-Jones, known as "the Old Grey Mare —
wise and kind".

It was the duty of Senior padres to care for their
juniors. They did their best to ensure that junior
padres who went with fighting troops fitted in. "The
only odd number I ever had", says one former Senior
padre, "was a man who complained about Officers'
messes as drunken ale-houses, and then was later
found himself under a mess table, completely out. He
was posted away."

Bill Story recalls that he used to call his chaplains
together, where possible, once a fortnight. "We had
religious papers or a training day. And of course it was
my duty to listen to any problems they might have."

He goes on, "Towards the end of the war I went to
five Corps with 25,000 troops. I had sixty-eight chaplains in my charge. My first task was to get to know
them. I called a conference from which emerged a
strong demand for a Quiet Day for prayer, meditation

and addresses. I found myself elected to lead this and it seemed well-received. A report filtered back . . . 'Thank God we have somebody we can talk to.' I found that what many people need is just to have somebody to express their worries to. In the end you may not have to give advice or practical help; they work things out for themselves and this is best."

When men were congregated in P.O.W. (Prisoner-of-War) camps they naturally came to know one another very well. Indeed, other people's little habits could drive you nearly mad — but you also got to know a person's real worth. Father Pat Rorke, now well into his eighties, with a long, humorous face, remembers with affection the "gang" in his last camp in Sumatra. He looks again at the words he wrote at the close of the war, bringing to mind the names and personalities with whom he shared the good and the bad. Even now he is deeply moved.

Turning the pages he recalls, "Yes, that one was always steady and unruffled; that one had a sharp tongue but a heart of gold; that one was the best interpreter and go-between we had; that was Dave who flogged my clothes and altar linen; that was 'the lad' — a nineteen-year-old, full of ulcers but always game and unafraid; and there was Jock — he had half my blanket and I used to retrieve this during my malaria spells . . ."

There were "the Nips" too. "Poor little Sgt Ebinuma, a harmless but ineffective little chap, worried by authority. There was 'King Kong', a dangerous fanatic for the letter of the law, not really unjust but madly severe. There was 'the Pig', better forgotten; there was 'the Chinaman', an amusing rogue who bought a wooded hill and then found the wood would not burn. There was 'the basher' who came near to killing our 'Skipper' and was carted off by the kampei for long and severe punishment. And there was Hiroka, a grand chap – good to us."

And Father Pat will never forget camp two, where so many men lay dying. "Here the fundamental nobility of human nature shone out in an amazing way. In the so-called hospital, a bare barn, men lay on boards along each side. A few grumbled but the vast majority displayed a patience and courage that was memorable. The very sick lay on camp beds down the middle. 'The middle' – that dread phrase, which spoke a sorrowful language, for very few who went there ever left the camp alive again, as they well knew.

"Many lads used to come to that place to bring small delicacies for their pals, and I have seen them sitting by sick men for an hour or more, with the patience of a mother, feeding them with a spoon. And it is tragic to remember that it was usually all in vain. But it was surely not passed over in the Great Book . . ."

4

Initiatives

Padres in war time found themselves doing unusual things. Geoffrey Harding says, "I ran a mobile NAAFI (Navy, Army and Air Force Institute) at one time . . . account after a fortnight . . . 6 pence out!" He emphasizes that there had to be much improvisation in France and Holland.

Sometimes initiative was considerable. Father Joe Gill served in Greece and Crete, and was responsible for more than thirty R.A.F. N.C.O.s and airmen getting to the boats in Crete before the Germans had overrun the island. They had become separated from their Commanding Officer, and Father Joe took charge and worked out a route over the mountains to the harbour. Now a small, spare figure, advanced in years, but still with sharp, bright eyes, Father Joe remembers events with perfect clarity but is unimpressed by his own involvement.

Humorously, Bill Story recalls being one night with rear H.Q. vehicles when their column became separated. The Post Corporal came up, saluted and said, "Will you take charge, sir – I seem to have got us in a muddle." Bill led the column for the remainder of the night and eventually caught up with the main party just after dawn. He was able to bring the C.O. news as to the position of one of his companies. "He seemed surprised", says Bill wryly, "that I could do anything useful."

There were of course hundreds of similar incidents of padres taking initiative. Many acquired new skills during the years of war – learning to drive, to fly and, according to H. Morley Rattenbury, "enjoying my single appearance as a stand-up comic on the stage of the Palace Theatre, Blackpool."

Men grew alert to notice new uses for familiar objects. One padre says of Far Eastern P.O.W. camp life – "We discovered that the latex from rubber trees was a good substitute for adhesive tape, for sores and ulcers." And a padre in a German P.O.W. camp recalls the importance of the string which surrounded the welcome Red Cross parcels. "This string gave us washing-lines, bootlaces, lashing, netting for basket-ball goals and potato skips, wonderful soft brooms and, if you were clever, slippers. This string was the envy of the Germans."

Somewhere to hold services was a priority, and not everyone was as fortunate as the crew of *H.M.S. Rodney*, blessed with its beautiful St Christopher's chapel, with its three stained-glass portholes and natural oak.

Eric Alsop stresses, "Necessity was definitely the mother of invention in those days. I held services in hangars, below decks, in the converted bike and paint shop of a parachute-packing plant, and under the blue dome of heaven on the back of my truck."

Padre Fisk tells us that in June 1942 while with 321 Wing MEF (Military Expeditionary Force) he "hired the cinema in the town nearby for Sunday evening service". Naval chaplain Hywell Evans celebrated

Eucharist on a street-corner café table on a Mediterranean island.

When servicemen were in an isolated place for any length of time, there was incentive to build a church. Ronald Martin recalls, "We furnished a church in the desert at Khormaksar which was on the model of the station church at Boscombe Down, to which local churches contributed linen, etc. It was furnished by workshops on the station." Vincent Parkin remembers making a church from a barn, with vases formed from shell cases and kneelers from sandbags, and Eric Mantle, also R.A.F., recalls churches built from petrol cans.

The Singapore Race Club church was put up in the Singapore Race Club stand, the shell hole in the stand being stuffed with mattresses and the altar being part of the original bar. Henry Babb, as a P.O.W., helped in the building of two chapels – one converting the box office of a Chinese cinema and the other at Chungkai, making a chapel from scratch with bamboo and rattan.

Christopher Ross, in the P.O.W. camp at Bang Pong, Siam, told of his struggles with the Japanese to obtain materials with which to build a church. The building was reluctantly allowed; then the church was pulled down. He wrote later, "You could judge the temper of things by the Japanese attitudes towards our church! A good story could be written about the number of times we built and moved our church. It was made of bamboo and dried leaves."

Yet Herbert Davies tells of how, in Shamshuipo camp, he finally convinced the Japanese that Easter was a great and glorious festival in our religion, and they permitted flowers to be put in the church.

One of the most famous churches to be constructed was St George's Church, Chechiban, near Tmimi in the Western Desert. This was the brainchild of Padre Dick Rudgard who, in a quiet period after the Battle of Alamein, decided to get a church built from scratch, using only materials lying around.

In January 1943 he wrote to his wife: "I seem busier now than when we were in battle. All the mornings I am visiting units and chaplains. In the afternoons I am building a church of stone with voluntary help." Soon he was writing, "My little church is going up well. The walls are three foot high and soon we shall be grappling with the problems of the windows. I think I shall use circular oil drums with the ends cut out and build up round them."

Then the church was reported as being five foot high, and Dick was writing, "I have just been digging out an iron girder from an old Italian dugout to go across the top of the door and carry stone on top." By February the church was open, though the roof was not yet on. There was "A lovely view of a deep wadi and the sea in the distance".

Rudgard wrote enthusiastically of the opening services and described the furnishings. "The Sappers have made a lovely stone altar, and for seats we are using kerosene tins covered with sandbags. On the altar I had two bowls of wild flowers, a cross and two olive-wood candlesticks. My church bells are three shell cases cut different lengths, made of brass, hit with a mallet and they sound very well . . ."

At last the roof was on, and a little low sanctuary

wall complete, with the sanctuary floor of crazy paving. A plaque in beaten metal was cemented in. It read:

To the glory of God
1st Armoured Division 1942–3

In these ways the service padres used their ingenuity to provide worthy sanctuaries for worshippers, and tried to make them as beautiful as possible. Ross Hook remembers deciding that "a white ensign over a table made a good frontal for worship".

Herbert Davies managed to get hymn books and Bibles through the good offices of a sympathetic Japanese Christian interpreter, known as Cardiff Joe. He quietly brought in books from Kowloon when he could. He also brought them a fine altar cross from St Andrew's church in Kowloon, which was placed on the altar in the camp each Sunday and cared for during the week. After the Japanese surrender, the cross was returned to St Andrew's.

Similarly, Raymond Bowers tells how they had no chalice in his German P.O.W. camp. "Arrangements were made for us to visit a Lutheran Bishop in Munich and he presented us with an enormous chalice and paten suitable for a cathedral."

Back in World War I, the Rev. Harry Blackburne had urged padres to "make reverent experiments and to celebrate at any time". During World War II, this idea was very much taken up. It seemed inevitable. W. H. Miller, travelling with Wingate's Chindits in Burma, wrote home, "As regards religious work, I am always experimenting".

When death so often threatened, and men's movements were so uncertain, most padres seized opportunities for religious practices. Ronald Bradwell recalls "the spontaneousness of Communion services; these revealed the folly of barriers erected in peace. I was the only chaplain on board the troop carrier *Empress of Australia* and I offered communion to all Protestants."

Sometimes the men themselves made the first move. Robert Clements, R.A.F., tells of an occasion about ten days before the Battle of Alamein. An Intelligence Officer at Advanced Air HQ approached him. "There is a Hurricane Squadron five miles south of Burg El Arab . . . photographic recce low level over the Axis lines . . . they've had a lot of casualties, including their C.O. We had his Second in today on promotion to command. They would like to see a chaplain." Clements says, "I went and saw the new C.O. – about twenty-two, very Oxbridge in manner. He said, 'We would like a service, we've lost a lot of pilots lately. We don't want hymns and sermons, just Holy Communion.' The pilots came, nineteen of them, kneeling in the sandy dust of the mess tent. So very young . . . not for them the thrill of combat . . . they flew through a hail of fire a few hundred feet above the foe, working their cameras. It was very moving. They knew the probabilities and entrusted themselves to God. A week later, seven had gone . . . twelve left and still in action . . ."

In his Javanese P.O.W. camp, Catholic Father Pat Rorke suggested to the C. of E. padre that he should have the conducting of the "one religious service a week" that was allowed, since he had the greater number of congregation.

"I decided I would offer Holy Mass unobtrusively in a corner. I said Mass in a lean-to shed, built by a lad called Peter. It was put up outside the windows of the barracks, and Pete used to hang a blanket across the window and clear his few effects from the board which he used for a bed. Here I offered the Holy Sacrifice. The lads in the barracks were busy devouring their rice nearby, quite unaware of my presence, and filling the air with their rich service language. Christ was on the altar and glad to be so near His brethren, who surely received a blessing as they sat at their watery dinner.

"When we moved to Batavia – the end of the reasonable times – we were determined we would not be deprived of Holy Communion at Easter. It was arranged that twelve lads should gather in one of the more remote cubicles in the barracks, each day, to hear Mass and communicate, and another twelve would meet me outside afterwards, when I would give them Communion as they stood, mingling with the crowd. We changed rendezvous each time and by the time Easter Week was over, all English-speaking Catholics had made their Easter duties. The C. of E. padre had a narrow escape, for one of his services had to break up unceremoniously, and he and two others scrambled out through a window on the ground floor . . ."

As the war continued, a new ecumenism took root slowly. One first war chaplain once wrote: "An Englishman does not give a pin what a man is, so long as he is genuine. He will come to a service if it appeals to him and the padre is manly – biretta or Salvation Army hat amuse him equally. He does not care whether a man wears vestments or a surplice so long as he is a man."

This may have been true of the service personnel in World War II but seems to have developed only gradually in the thinking of the padres. Moreover, the new liberalism of ecclesiastical behaviour did not go down well with everyone back in England. Presumably tales filtered back of unorthodox practices, which upset some. Ronald Martin recalls with some amusement a letter written to a church newspaper in England expressing the view that "Service chaplains were becoming lawless and irresponsible", and recommending that on being demobbed they should be "retrained by experienced parish priests".

The experienced parish priests in the Forces took a dim view of this chap who "sharpened up his pen to protect the faithful stay-at-homes from wicked servicemen".

Another line from some verses circulating at the time on this topic spoke affectionately of "the chaplains, unsuspecting, who continued at their play, holding services in NAAFIs, in a shaggy sort of way . . ."

Despite such strictures, the padres continued to employ all their ingenuity to fulfil their vocation and make available the resources of the Christian Church.

The holding of Communion or saying of Mass often presented practical difficulties, particularly in remote areas or within the P.O.W. camps. In these circumstances, various substances were utilized for the elements, and it was a case of this or nothing. Bill Story says: "In the later stages of the retreat to Alamein, supplies became difficult and I had to use army biscuits in place of bread and cold tea for wine." Raymond Bowers in Germany used "black bread and some scrounged wine". Herbert Davies in Shamshuipo used "wafers made from rice flour and for wine, water in which raisins had been soaked". Christopher Ross, in Siam, used "for bread, inferior canteen biscuits or thin rice-flour cake. For wine, boiled water, weak tea, coffee, coconut milk, brown sugar water, lime juice . . ." Australian padre "Happy Harry" Thorpe, on the Burma-Siam railway, used rice bread and pomelo juice.

Neville Metcalfe speaks of the Communion service held on Whit Sunday in the vicinity of Imphal, in the evacuation of Burma. "We had army biscuits as wafers and some local whisky procured from a friendly Naga 'head hunter' tribe and used in lieu of the usual communion wine. Despite the fact that it had been much watered down, it took the silver lining off the silver sports trophy cup which had been pressed into service as a chalice. Stomachs already weakened by attacks of dysentery were alas further aggravated."

Two padres did startling things about which they had no qualms. W. H. Miller, with Wingate in Burma, left a record of a time when the men were "very thirsty, they had not found the stream they had been led to believe existed. All went thirsty for two days and nights. I decided to share out the sacramental wine and wafer – it was a mere taste. It seemed the Christian thing to do. I would do it again. The men were pathetically grateful . . ."

And Father Pat Rorke in his Far Eastern camp put

his Bible and breviaries on the market to ensure that the men had paper in which to roll their tobacco – no shortage of shag, but shortage of paper. "Ten cigarette papers from a page of my Bible. Everyone was happy except for a few straitlaced Dutch Lutherans!"

Scraping money together in the camp to obtain food and nursing extras called forth all the ingenuity Father Pat could summon. "Prices on the native market were soaring fantastically and our so-called 'pay' was useless to cope with this. Hence we carried on a continual process of selling everything we had to the natives.

"We had already disposed of watches and rings to the guards. So we then sold our clothes, our blankets, the skirting of mosquito nets if we owned such luxuries, and some lads made themselves a pair of trunks from sacking and disposed of everything else. Men who went to the jungle to cut down trees for the cookhouse fires acted as agents, taking commission on the sales.

"As the only functioning chaplain in that area, I had many calls on my money. Sick and needy P.O.W.s cast hopeful eyes on the padre. I looked with a critical eye on what else could be flogged. My vestments! My altar wine was going and I did not think I would say Mass again until we were free. Then I could always get fresh vestments. So my alb, made for me by good Sisters in Glasgow, fetched 300 guilders. I was sore at parting with it. Two sets of vestments made in Batavia went next. Altar cloths went the same way, and finally my reversible chasuble that I had when I first joined up. The proceeds from all this proved invaluable soon after, when I was moved back to the base camp to look after the sick and dying. I had up to now kept back my breviary and a missal that had belonged to my brother. Now they all went. Then I did become a poor man – nothing else left to flog!"

5

Prisoners-of-War

According to Father Pat Rorke – "Prisoner-of-war life was summed up in one word – WAITING."

Frustration was the main emotion of the padres incarcerated in P.O.W. camps. There was frustration that they were not moving along with the troops to the desired end of victory. And for many, frustration that they did not feel they were able to fulfil to the utmost the vocation they had offered.

The Germans proved loath to post chaplains to Other Ranks camps, since they had no wish to raise the morale of prisoners, which they thought the chaplains would certainly try to do. They desired to keep morale low, so that inmates would more easily accept political propaganda. It was not until about 1943, when our Forces had taken considerable numbers of German prisoners, that some attention was paid in this matter to the details of the Geneva Convention. Thus there could be, as at one time in Oflag VIIC in Germany in July 1940, as many as forty padres and eighty doctors. Also, many chaplains, as non-combatants, expected to be repatriated when taken prisoner. Rumours often reassured them but turned out to be false. Some, like John F. O. Bown, were fortunate, but many others remained in the camps until the cessation of hostilities.

Of course Officers' camps could use good padres.

"Jock" Ellison Platt, one of the early British arrivals at the "bad boys" camp, the notorious Colditz, made quite a name for himself. Comparatively middle-aged, he stood as a father figure and was a popular preacher with a good understanding of human nature. His diary recorded the minutiae of camp life, which became incredibly significant in the claustrophobia of imprisonment.

Says one padre, "Diaries in P.O.W. hands were highly suspect. The only chance of avoiding confiscation was to omit everything that might irritate the Germans, so that pages could be safely read and stamped as innocuous by the camp censors on their periodical searches and inspections." Many wrote accounts of their imprisonment at the end of the war, while events were still sharp in their minds. Raymond Bowers, one of the luckless who jumped at Arnhem, with the 10th Battalion of the 4th Parachute Brigade, and was captured and evacuated to Germany, recorded his captivity.

"I was specifically asked to go with the wounded and not to try to escape. It was a long three-day trip with a lot of hanging about. We first went to Mossburg which was a transit hospital with Stalag VIIA beside it. It looked very forbidding when we entered through large wired gates with searchlights shining down, and heard the gates clang behind us. A new episode had begun."

There was no point in the padres being "uppish". Bowers described "A rather cold start. We were herded into a huge hall and our clothes taken for delousing. We were left naked till morning."

As the Rev. John McKie Hunter, padre with the

51st Highland Division, is said to have commented: "It is difficult to adopt a conventional attitude to the person squatting beside one on a pole above a latrine trench . . . in such circumstances, real conversations have a habit of developing."

Raymond Bowers was quickly visited by an Australian padre and asked, *sotto voce*, "Do you want to work or be idle?" In this blunt query, Bowers was lucky since he was anxious to get to the working camps in Munich where he thought he could be more useful.

Achieving this and actually getting to Munich proved a devious procedure. In his parachute descent, Bowers had sustained a fractured foot, and though this was satisfactorily operated upon in a Dutch hospital, it was decided he must now suffer another "phoney" operation, which would conveniently detain him for a while in a ward. His ankle was put back in plaster and he began the waiting game. "I was told a plan was in motion to get me to Munich but it would take time – and a lot of ciggies.

"Hanging about became very boring. I challenged more plastercast lads to a steeplechase over the beds. In no time at all, a book had been made and we were off. It was all very silly but it made for a lot of laughter. By now my leg was very uncomfortable, not on account of any pain, but because my plaster was harbouring a host of bedbugs."

Word came through that a place had been found for him in Munich. His plaster was cut off and he walked five miles to the station. "It was so strange to be outside. In Munich I settled down to a rewarding ministry. It was a non-military work camp – snow shifting, roof-tiling, street-cleaning and, very popular, working in the brewery. There was a certain amount of sabotage. I was able to visit ten other camps in the area, accompanied by a guard and an interpreter who was meant to see that the padre did not spread sedition. I visited camps in Augsburg and in Bad Tolz up in the mountains.

"My ideal had always been to get away from the Officers' Mess and among the men. Here as a P.O.W. padre I was more satisfied with the opportunities." Sadly, there was a certain irony in the opportunities; early in 1945, in a British thousand-bomber raid, his camp lost nine of their own men. "With dead from another camp, a mass funeral was held at Munich cemetery. The Germans gave them full military honours."

Bowers recalls how he later learned that his wife, on hearing him "reported missing", put an advertisement in a London paper, asking for information. "She got all kinds of stories – I had been seen swimming the Rhine, and also at the window of a house in Oosterbeek shouting and cursing graphically."

--◦•‡※‡•◦--

A padre not fortunate enough either to get repatriated or, for some years, to a work camp, was John King, captured in France on 12th June 1940. Still a tall, elegant man, he then accepted that "there was now no more anxiety; no more planning; no responsibility; no effort. We had made a run for it. Now initiative was out of our hands. We suddenly felt very tired."

Many must have echoed the comments at the beginning of his immaculately kept diary: "So here I am in prison, with a tin number round my neck and no hair on my head; guarded by high walls and barbed wire and by soldiers with rifles, revolvers and machine gun towers. For how long, I wonder? And will our people know that we are safe, or shall we be posted as 'missing' indefinitely?"

Through a window he could see the river — "a symbol of the time we are wasting here behind these walls, where one thousand three hundred intelligent and active beings do little but crawl about like invalids, lest we grow too hungry before the next meal. It is perfectly awful how hungry one does get and remain constantly . . ."

Food looms large in all diaries and records. "Just enough here to keep us going at the slow pace demanded and with no reserves. We would like exercise to whip up the circulation but it would also whip up the appetite too and we can't afford to do that."

These diaries set out clearly the various problems of camp life — hunger, depression, the inevitable rumours and lack of reliable news, overcrowding, lack of letters. And being cooped up with other padres of various denominations was not necessarily a beatific experience.

Yet there were mitigating events — excitement when letters finally arrived; friendships made, parole walks, library work and, for John King, an accomplished musician, the interest and achievement of forming choirs and maintaining a musical standard in worship. There was a determination "not to be got down". Overcoming hunger, particularly in early camp days, was often a matter of resolutely turning the mind and hands to specific activity. "I have spent a great deal of today embroidering my name on a grey blanket in blue wool unwound from an old sock discarded by a Second Lieutenant", wrote King.

The arrival of the Red Cross parcels was a high spot. Not only most welcome food had been packed, but useful comforts – scarves, gloves, socks. Best of all was the thought that someone had cared about them and had been thinking of them.

John's diary records the formation of "the University of Laufen". Proudly he recalls that this was staffed by the members of the Oflag. "We had very high standards when you remember that we did not possess a single text book", he says. A long list of subjects could be studied "from metallurgy to metaphysics, book-keeping to bee-keeping. Apart from utilitarian benefits, these lectures prevented us from going to seed and becoming complete cabbages."

A moving paragraph in the diaries reveals some of the inner longings of one padre; a bout of home-sickness summoned up poignant memories.

"Although I have become almost contented, there is always the danger of being caught between wind and water by some flash of the imagination. Yesterday it was the sudden remembrance of the big easy chairs at home. Here we have a solid four-legged stool which has to be carried around . . . nor is it only an arm-chair's comfort; there is something about it which stands for many things beside – spaciousness of living, serenity, fastidiousness . . . other things I long for too. Thin glass to drink from, food that needs a knife and not a spoon; a bed wide enough to turn in, with a pillow, not a canvas bag stuffed with straw. Music to listen to, a telephone to use. Lawns to walk on. The feel of a cassock and above all — space. Not nine in a room to sleep, eat, work and play; not five hundred on a landing, nor over a thousand in a courtyard. But three or four on a carpeted floor. And the aisles of Durham . . ."

Bursts of joy came sometimes. Out on a parole walk they went into some churches. "We have no colour in prison, just ubiquitous khaki, grey and cement. Only our views are beautiful. The chief joy of the churches was their colour — the flamboyant rococo . . ." They walked through fields of powdered December snow. "For our room window I picked a handful of open countryside — briony, nightshade, birch catkins and some pussy willows with buds like pearls."

He seized every opportunity to pursue his vocation, even holding a secret Mass in the hospital very early on Sunday mornings. And, he says, "One of my really profitable jobs was my intercession list — a joyful contrast to the general crippling effect of captivity."

—••‡ ✂ ‡••—

Thousands of miles away, other padres suffered the deprivations, indignities and pains of the Far Eastern camps. Among such was Herbert L. O. Davies, taken prisoner after the seventeen days of fighting in Hong Kong, in December 1941. He kept a brief diary, which he hid when searches took place. A dignified, upright, composed man, Davies speaks of his privilege in giving spiritual comfort to the troops in Shamshuipo camp. "Here", he says, "starvation rations, complete lack of drugs and medical supplies, insanitary conditions —

the camp was on earth buckets — brought about disease, incredible suffering and a high death-rate. On one day in October 1942 I took the burial service for nine men."

As always, food figures largely in his diary. "Meat with night meal — a great event" is one scrawl. "Bread rolls and dripping for tea" — "rice and egg plant" read other extracts. Red Cross parcels here were very few and far between. "When one arrived in the autumn, the men were so excited they asked to hold a Harvest Festival."

Davies was faithful in celebrating the Church's year and made a point of impressing on the Japanese the sacredness of the Christian festivals. He did his utmost to get them to exempt men from working parties on these days.

"Because of poor food many people developed swollen ankles and legs due to an almost totally rice diet. As malnutrition increased there were outbreaks of beri beri, when the men suffered from bad feet. They had this pain known as 'dancing feet' or 'electric feet', when they could not keep still. It stopped them sleeping; they became like walking skeletons."

Life was often tediously slow and no news came. The diary records small domestic tasks carried out to pass the time. "Washed surplices; ironed shirt and shorts. Kneaded bread. Cleaned onions. Cut grass. Marked out quoit court. Quiz and spelling bee. Bottled raisin wine."

A noticeable feature in all such diaries is the manner in which entries combine in an unemotional way the detailing of horrifying events together with comments on trivial occurrences.

"Chinese shot on bamboo pier . . . made to kneel, lunged at with bayonets when he fell into the water; then they put a bullet through his head. Those of us who saw this atrocity felt sick but completely helpless. Concert in the evening quite good."

Sometimes a single chilling line appears. "Dec. 1942. A story is going round of human meat being sold in Hong Kong."

One simple incident indicates the tensions in the camp and the way in which, unsuspectingly, one could easily get on the wrong side of the Commandant, known in this camp as "Fat Pig".

Herbert was engaged to be married, his fiancée an Army Nurse interned in Stanley camp. They were allowed to write one postcard each month – block capitals, no more than twenty-five words. Herbert had written to Mary early in 1944 – "Hoping this year will see us together". "Having handed this in, I was later ordered to report to the office of the Japanese Commandant, where I saw my card on his table. They had taken exception to something.

"The interpreter asked, 'Are you a Christian and do you speak the truth?' 'I hope so', I replied. Then he said, 'We keep a close watch on you – you are always moving round the camp talking to the men. Now if you will tell us how you got the information that the war is going to end this year, I will not punish you.'

"I was aghast. Like everyone else, I was confined behind the wire. I only went outside to bury the dead.

"I answered – 'Hope springs eternal in the human breast, if you know what that means.' 'Come off it,' said the interpreter, 'you know something – how and when did you get this information?' I repeated that I was simply hoping and that every war ends sometime. Finally, storming and bellowing, the Commandant called me a liar and bundled me out."

Herbert is very proud of his late wife, formerly Matron Mary Currie, Q.A. Matron of St Albert's Hospital. He believes that, at a time when hospital nurses went in fear of attack and rape, she probably saved her staff from atrocity by her conduct. When Japanese soldiers burst into her hospital, she spoke pointedly, with dignity and courage, of her under-standing that Japanese soldiery were civilized. She persuaded the leader to accompany her to a ward where a Japanese officer had died that morning. He had been laid out very respectfully, according to Japanese custom, with the Japanese flag wrapped round the middle of his body. This impressed the soldiers and they went away.

Amazing resources were summoned up by some padres. Herbert recollects one who insisted on singing the national anthem every Sunday after service and was consistently publicly flogged for this.

Herbert is convinced that "spirit was everything". Some men and women kept going in spite of all the trials, while some folded. "I remember one chap, a university man, they said he died of lice but I think that, sadly, he just gave up."

Lice and rice were both trials. A colourful padre, Tom Pugh, later Canon of Lincoln, left a record of an awful psychological malady which afflicted a camp in Formosa. "We just lived on rice; rice for breakfast and lunch and supper, and after three years the men developed an invincible revulsion and could not swallow the rice. In one day I buried nine men who had been virtually choked to death by the rice. That night, under cover of darkness, I went round the camp explaining to the men that this rice represented a bridge between ourselves and our homes and we had to eat. I thought I could help them to swallow the rice. Tomorrow when it comes, I told them, instead of saying 'Here comes this . . . rice again', I want you to say, 'For these and all His mercies may God's Holy Name be praised'. If you do this, I will guarantee you will be able to swallow the rice. It worked and many lived."

Christopher Ross wrote of his experiences in Japanese camps after the fall of Singapore, when he was marched to Changi camp in February 1942, the first of many moves. He thought it "a grand opportunity for a chaplain". On going to Thailand his battalion had no provision for a padre, but he wrote, "I wangled it and went. It was a never-to-be-forgotten journey! On arrival in Bang Pong, I tried to establish my position as padre, but failed and was compelled to do the work of a coolie for twenty-five cents a day. Later I was allowed to take services, but hymnsheets were confiscated as the Japanese thought I was distributing allied propaganda leaflets."

He grasped that they were the advance party for the Burma railway. "The policy in these camps was 'overcrowd, underfeed, overwork, beat'." The men worked in distressing conditions and staged a strike. He wanted to stand with them but on the advice of the Senior officer did not. "It was my job to go pleading to the Jap Commandant for improvements. I kept getting threatened and kicked out of the office. I thought my end had come when the Commandant one day drew his sword and swung it round my head. But the men did win a partial victory and beatings ceased for a few days.

"The morale of the men was marvellous. Services were curtailed and we were not allowed to sing in the huts or at services, and could not pray for England or an allied victory. All my 'religious effects' were taken from me. The officers and men were very kind to me at this moment − instead of the Church breaking, it seemed to gather a spiritual strength hitherto unknown . . ."

Patrick Rorke recalls the uncertainty of camp life. "There is no denying that the war may go on and on, food and conditions may get worse; there may be a pogrom and all the camp be put under collective punishment. You may accidentally fall foul of a guard; others may be in trouble and you can do nothing; scanty privileges may be stopped and help for the sick may be penalized."

Gerald O'Connell Fitz-Gerald was the only British naval chaplain to become a prisoner of the Japanese. After the sinking of *H.M.S. Exeter*, he was picked up and taken to Macassar, where he stayed until his release in September 1945.

Now over eighty years old, he still speaks with amazement at what he considers the miraculous manner in which he acquired the books needed for the pursuance of his priestly vocation. Naturally, taken from the water, everything had gone. The survivors of the *Exeter* were required to demolish a small house, and among the rubble a sailor found a small, backless copy of the Book of Common Prayer and Hymns Ancient and Modern, bound together. This was surprising because there were no English residents in Macassar, though the Dutch residents were excellent linguists.

As Gerald says – "We were halfway there, but still no Bible." He goes on to relate how only one further P.O.W. came to camp after his own time of arrival. This was an Australian airman shot down in the north of Celebes, who had been kept in Menado but then sent to Macassar. As this man was being marched to the ship en route, an old Indonesian patriarch ran up to him from the crowd and stuffed into his hand a copy of the Authorized Version of the Bible. This was subsequently given to Gerald O'Connell Fitz-Gerald. "It certainly seemed a miracle", he says. When released in 1945, he broke and buried the champagne glass and the saucer which he had used as his chalice and paten during his captivity.

—··❧❉❧··—

At the end of the European war, a padre with the 32nd Casualty Clearing Station entered Belsen, the "horror camp". Of the fifty thousand people herded there, when the C.C.S. entered, between seven and ten thousand lay dead and thousands of others dying. Father Michael Morrison, S.J., worked with a Polish priest caring for the dying in this dreadful place. Father Michael possessed the only stock of oil, and he described the joy and gratitude of internees receiving the sacraments — "One was conscious of being members of a living unified Church and of the bonds which held us together."

One diary, written immediately after the signing of the peace in 1945, encapsulated a bitter journey made as soon as the P.O.W.s had left by air for home. Henry Babb, padre to the East Surreys, joined a party of Australian officers and representatives of the Commonwealth Graves Commission, to seek and identify all the cemeteries and graves which marked in tragic fashion the line of the infamous Burma railway — 415 kilometres from Non Pladuk in Thailand to Thanhyuzuyat in Burma — "The Kwai graves".

Henry had served alongside the prisoners who worked on the railway from 1942. "I was able to take at least one or two services during the week and on Sunday Holy Communion to any fellow prisoners when they got back from work on the railway. And I took services in the hospital hut in either a camp on the line or at the base, Chungkai." He also buried four hundred of his comrades.

The war had now ended but Henry was reliving sad events as he set off in a diesel-powered railcar to search for the 10,549 graves on or near the railway of death. And daily he wrote in his diary. He was constantly pondering "what a terrible time the lads had here". They spent hours searching through jungle grass, so that they could chart the graves and ensure that the little cemeteries or lone resting places were orderly and peaceful. He found it a great ordeal. After returning to England he burned his diary without looking at it again.

He knew he had allowed it to be copied by a friend

in Bangkok but had not realized a copy still existed. One had gone into the hands of a sympathetic young Japanese who had acted as interpreter on the sad journey searching for the graves. Over forty years after it was written, this Japanese friend tracked him down with the diary copy and Henry re-read it. "I would want to have a spirit of forgiveness," he said, "but I could never forget."

One chaplain relates a story with its own sting in the tail. The Senior British officer in a Far Eastern P.O.W. camp was unable to comply with the demand of the Camp Commandant for details of the work skills of the men in the Officer's unit. "Can't do", he said firmly — "Not allowed." On pain of death he refused to part with these details. The situation being made totally plain, the Officer called the men together and said, in a matter of fact manner, "I am going to be shot tomorrow; I cannot give the information they want – and no more will you." The following day he was taken out and shot. The men were in a turmoil. Then, to their amazement, they found that the Japanese had erected a small cairn over the Officer's grave and above it had written "In memory of a brave Officer". They themselves were not asked again about their jobs and heard no more of the matter.

Father Pat Rorke speaks movingly of the strange peace that descended on "his" P.O.W. camp when peace was declared.

"The news of victory was broken to us about 22nd August. I felt ready to sing a Nunc Dimittis. There was nothing similar to the frenzies associated with V-days at home. There was no shouting, or rushing about. Just a feeling of indescribable relief. A great quietness came into our lives. It was as though we had been living in the midst of continuous noise and clanging and blaring of metal and shouting of men. And then there had come a sudden quiet. The Nips took themselves off and interned themselves in their own barracks . . . We strolled about the camp until one in the morning, smoking under the moon. The sense of freedom came like a balm upon our souls. You would turn a corner and find three lads sitting round a fire frying fish in the middle of the night. And no guards to interfere. No one who has not been a P.O.W. can appreciate what that means . . ."

—•◦•—

6

Their Message

"Kill to save the world!" This declamation allegedly rang out from a bishop in Westminster Abbey during World War I. A rather different attitude prevailed in the Second World War. In June 1944, Padre Frederick Llewelyn Hughes, Senior Chaplain, 8th Army, stated:

"Chaplains have not been asked to harness the Christian Faith to military operations. Militant ranting is much disliked. We were asked to make our men as Christian as we could, to preach the Word of Christ faithfully, for it is true; to minister the Sacraments for their own proper effects; to bring men to God that He might make them good . . ."

These views are echoed by others who remember their own chaplaincies in World War II. Bill Story speaks for many when he agrees: "I never once received any suggestions as to what should be preached, nor did I hear of any other chaplain doing so. We were free to preach the 'pure Gospel' to the limits of our ability."

This they did in their individual ways. Mass was said by Catholic and High Anglican clergy wherever possible. Parade services, though compulsory, were conducted, so far as possible, with dignity and order. Francis Cocks, who became Chaplain-in-Chief, Royal Air Force, recalls "Huge parade services at Cranwell in the early days with over a thousand in the hangar church". He admits to problems. "For many R.A.F. chaplains, the dichotomy was between the safety we enjoyed on the ground and the nightly peril faced by aircrew, especially on bomber stations. Unlike the Army and Navy we seldom shared the same dangers except perhaps in the Western Desert and in the Far East collapse, and to a limited extent in Europe . . ."

Neville Metcalfe remembers how they sank down exhausted, at Whitsun 1942, in the vicinity of Imphal. "My chaplain's equipment was at a minimum – it had gone over a cliff in the dark. However, with an orange box as altar, prayer books reduced to fifty and no music, yet the service went with a swing. Generals Wavell and Alexander, who had 'dropped in', attended and stayed for Communion."

Many remember clearly, or wrote down, the texts and themes of sermons delivered in those days. These were obviously intended to encourage and uphold the troops and to deal with some of their questions. Robert Clements notes that he spoke upon "What is man?" – "The deep meaning of freedom" – "Faith in a world like this" – "Jesus the Man" – "Christ in the heart".

Sermons in camps had to be written out beforehand and submitted to the camp commandant for a stamp of approval. Herbert L. Davies in Shamshuipo detailed in his diary his sermon themes. These included: "Paul and Silas in prison" – "Going the second mile" – "The Light of the World" – "The thorn in the flesh" – "The Lost sheep" – and some poignant words from the Book of Job: "I would not lose hope, however long my service, waiting for my relief to come."

Christopher Ross wrote a sermon just for Japanese

consumption. "I was at least trying to get the Christian message over to them."

Bill Story who, as a Senior Chaplain, was constantly travelling, gives two delightful tales of services-with-a-difference. One which he attended was held for Indian Christians and took place in a farmhouse. The Indians had decorated the room with wild flowers from ceiling to floor, and put chains of coloured flowers slung across from side to side. "It would have put many a Harvest Festival to shame." The Bishop addressed the men through two interpreters and gave a blessing. It was for all a day of great joy.

Another day, while driving down a desert road south of Gaza, he came upon a camp of West African Pioneers doing road repairs. Their African Sgt Major, on seeing a chaplain, asked if there could be a service.

"Then," said the Sgt Major, eyes gleaming, "we can have a war dance in honour of the word of God." So Bill stayed. "I held a traditional service and then watched the ceremonial dance which went on for half an hour. Men postured, stamped, clapped, sang and chanted in chorus. It was fascinating."

Services did not always go according to plan. Tom Warner recalls that, whilst in mid-flow of a sermon in Sullom Voe in the Shetlands, a sheep stuck its nose inside the door and went "Baa", thus effectively terminating that message. Likewise Gwilym Williams recalls a service in the canteen of a naval training establishment. The war was not then going well and people were rather downcast. "My theme", says Gwilym, "was 'Lift up your hearts!' I was just getting to the core and asking people 'What are we going to do about it?' when a voice over the tannoy in the canteen cried 'Up Spirits!' – the call for the daily rum ration of those times. This brought the house down."

Patrick Rorke remembers an evening when he was talking on "prayer". His audience in the jungle seemed restless. Afterwards he discovered that a tree behind him held a dozen acrobatic monkeys. Who could compete?

One anecdote tells of a service in the Protestant Cathedral in Cyprus. The O.C., a humble man, preferred to sit at the back. But the troops did not appreciate this at all – they liked to see their officers up front. They said they kept expecting to hear a roar from behind – "Sgt Major, tell that man to get his hair cut!" Meekly, on hearing this, the O.C. agreed to move.

A service was arranged for the Yorkshire Hussars when stationed in Cyprus, in a village west of Nicosia. An abandoned church was offered as a regimental chapel. When Bill Story arrived for the service, he was surprised to see on the vestry table a copy of a thriller by Dorothy Sayers, *The Nine Tailors*. A man rushed in, grabbed the book and rushed out. He climbed a ladder and, setting himself astride the rounded barrel roof with the book in one hand and a wooden mallet in the other, proceeded to ring the changes on six camel bells which had been tuned into a peal and hung in the empty bell turret. He could not proceed without the bell-ringing instructions contained in the thriller.

Padres learned to face the facts of life. Raymond Bowers, in his German camp, had a stove in his hut on which the men might cook if they had wood. This became scarce and even wood brought in might be confiscated. The Sunday evening service was held in the laundry, the largest available room, and one with chairs. To his surprise, Bowers found his congregations growing remarkably large.

"I mentioned this to the M.O. He smiled and said, 'Don't you realize – they only come for the firewood!' The next time I also helped by breaking up a chair and returning with two bits stuck up my trouser legs . . ."

A similar let-down afflicted Robert Clements on the escarpment at Gambut in Cyrenaica. There was a crowd of over two hundred men from a recently arrived Squadron. It was not a parade, the Adjutant had made that clear, but had promised to publicize it in Orders.

"The large company surprised and delighted me. They sang well and listened politely. At the end I said, 'If anyone would like a quiet word or a free copy of the gospels, or a New Testament with the R.A.F. crest . . . wait and see me.'

"To my surprise, all stayed and moved from their seats to form a queue six foot deep by the wall. Then the organizing Flight Sgt whispered, 'Sorry sir, I don't think they are waiting for you. We had the NAAFI wagon in today . . . the first beer for a month. We said it would be distributed after the service . . .'"

Nevertheless, services were held whenever possible. Says Gordon Brigg, "During a battle it was almost impossible to find time and place for even a brief Communion, let alone a service. A brief prayer with the gun crew was as much as I could hope for." And Tom Warner – "What relevance had a service consisting of three hymns, a Bible reading, prayers and an address, for R.A.F. men under canvas?"

All padres made utmost efforts to celebrate the great Christian festivals and this was usually appreciated by the troops. Diaries and memoirs stress the importance of Christmas, though the ambivalent nature of this celebration has to be acknowledged. For many serving troops, with little Christian background, it was a holiday and they would get the most from it. There was inevitably a lot of drunkenness as the day wore on. Bill Story was saddened when a Hindu officer commented to him, "What is this Christmas? I thought it was a religious festival." Bill says, "Of course he had not seen into any of the churches – only what went on in the streets and canteens."

The chaplains went to great lengths to see that the men had a good time, with extra rations and cigarettes, but also did their best to draw them to early services and to offer them the glorious Good News of the birth of Christ.

The musically-talented John King, in Laufen P.O.W. camp, produced a service of Nine Lessons and Carols, in all details following the pattern of the service he had loved at King's College, Cambridge. This involved arranging the service totally from memory and scoring the music, since they possessed no printed scores. Amazingly, a full orchestra was gathered together from camp residents, with instruments provided by the Red Cross. The Germans, with their reverence for good music, and the knowledge that large numbers of inmates would be for a time safely and harmlessly occupied, facilitated the provision of the instruments. John King was delighted with the result and so was everyone else. After effecting this in the Laufen camp,

King repeated it, under much less promising conditions, in his Polish camp at Schildberg. "A wonderful day", he wrote, "in spite of everything. I think this is one of the very best evangelistic services. The sweep of the Lessons is quite majestic."

In a small camp on the outskirts of Munich run by a Scottish Sgt Major, Raymond Bowers went to conduct a Christmas service. He wanted the entire camp to be present, and the Sgt Major declared it would have to be held outside, for lack of space. So they cleared an area and piled the snow feet high all round. "It was bitterly cold," remembers Bowers, "and I kept everything brief – a couple of carols, short prayers and readings, an address and a blessing. When we hurried back to the hut and were thawing out, I asked the Sgt Major if everything had gone off all right. 'Aye,' he said, 'but I thought, sir, the sermon was a wee bitty short . . .'"

Motives were often mixed, as with the vast numbers of carol singers round the camps on the promise of a special supper later. But the general mood was good, and the padres tried to inspire a true Christmas spirit. Bill Story travelled round scattered companies. He began at 5.00 A.M. on his motor bike, with fourteen assignments, ending up at 2.00 P.M. when he went to the mess to help with the men's dinners, in the traditional manner.

The ship *Penelope*'s assignment was the protection of British supply ships to Malta, and she escorted several convoys and survived several dive-bombing attacks. Christmas 1941 was approached by her captain and crew with apprehension. Would there be raids? But all was well, as reported by her chaplain,

John Inderwick Palmer. "We were able to start our midnight Communion Service to the accompaniment on the bosun's pipe of 'Raiders past' — the next best thing to angels singing 'Peace on earth, goodwill towards men . . . '"

Holy Week was less easy. "It's difficult to make much of it", wrote John King. "Good Friday — so unlike any other. Usually it is a day on which serenity, true proportion of outlook, a rock bottom reality are most nearly achieved than at any other time. Partly the problem here has been due to exterior circumstances — a crowd from which there is no escaping, a noisy room full of bottled beer, accordions and general squalor; such a change from the enfolding detachment of a Three Hours Service and all the privacy one wants on one's knees . . ."

On Easter Day he could be more cheerful. "A good day in spite of wind and rain — it fell to me to say 8.30 Mass. There were thirty-five communicants and as many again at 9.15. Matins at 10.15 and Evensong at 4. All crowded. The German Q.M. gave us the opportunity of buying Bavarian Easter cakes — a Paschal Lamb sat with a saucy look on his face and a bell round his neck on a golden ribbon. I had a letter from my wife, which is more than could happen on a Sunday in England."

Padres took seriously the instruction of men and women and their reception as communicants or church members. In October 1942, in Latafaya, an Army camp thirty miles to the south of Baghdad, Neville Metcalfe was able to present a group of men for the rite of Confirmation in the English Church in Baghdad.

When possible, formal Confirmation celebrations were held and visiting Bishops arrived. In the spring of 1943 Bill Story received a signal that the Bishop of Khartoum would be coming to Cyprus. It was rather awkward since the whole division would be up in the Troodos range carrying out important twelve-day exercises. How to get the men to their Confirmation? It needed a visit to the General.

The General told the A.D.M.S. (Assistant Director of Medical Services) "I hear that a Prince of the Church will be here . . . etc., etc. Padre Story will give you a list of sixty-five men, their names and units. You will arrange for them to become 'casualties' on the day and have them evacuated as a medical exercise by ambulance to the hospital in Nicosia. The hospital will house them for the night and see they have transport to the Cathedral the following day. They will be returned to their units the day after that as 'reinforcements'." All went well with this plan.

"The Bishop was a small man, not physically imposing," says Bill Story, "but he soon won all hearts. He told them he liked to speak to soldiers as he was a private soldier in the first great war. The Bishop had said, 'In fact I rose to the dizzy heights of Lance Corporal – but only for a week – then my stripe was taken away again!'

"All listened raptly to his simple message", goes on Bill. "As the Bishop said goodbye I passed him a message from a man who asked, 'How did you lose your stripe?' 'Oh, quite simple – my puttees came down on parade . . .' He left to thunderous cheers . . ."

Events could be slightly bizarre. Robert Clements relates how the Bishop of Jo'burg took a Confirmation service in a Tobruk cinema. "This cinema was crowded with airmen and also with soldiers. The service was impressive. Towards the end, the Sgt Major walked along the gangway and in a stage whisper called out, 'Have you been confirmed? If not, now's your chance to be done ... come on ...' A few followed him. A purist would be shocked by such casual participation in a solemn rite. I was at first, but reflected on the evangelical hymn which says, 'All the fitness He requireth is to feel your need of Him'."

Their Graces were equal to all for which they were called upon. In September 1942, the then Archbishop of Canterbury, William Temple, was invited by the Commander-in-Chief of the Navy to visit the Home Fleet. The Chaplain of the *King George V*, James Churchill Waters, serving under the esteemed Admiral Sir "Jack" Tovey, was given the job of meeting the Archbishop and went in a destroyer to Thurso to collect him. The journey to Scapa Flow was rough but the Archbishop, in the Captain's sea-cabin, appeared undisturbed.

The chaplain said, "The sailors would love to see you, sir". "Of course, I'll come", was the response and for the remainder of the trip the Archbishop was surrounded by sailors. He possessed marked and genial personality. When a barge arrived to take him to the *King George V*, something occurred which Chaplain Waters declared he had never seen before. "Instead of a formal departure with men at attention, the sailors crowded to the guardrails and cheered repeatedly and spontaneously. It was a heart-warming tribute to a great Christian."

Another episcopal tale comes from Tom Warner.

The Bishop of Aberdeen and Orkney responded willingly to an invitation to dedicate a church – the east end of a new gymnasium.

"We sent down a Blenheim for the old boy, then in his seventies. The pilot told him to stay where he was in the co-pilot's seat until the fans stopped turning. Perhaps he didn't hear – he got out on the wing – only to be blown off into my arms. Dressed in gaiters and black silk stockings and shoes with silver buckles, he cut a quaint caper. But everybody fell for him and he wanted the boys to take him on ops – but the Air Ministry wouldn't hear of it . . .

"Next morning a gale was blowing – 100 m.p.h. in squalls. The M.T. (Mechanical Transport) drove us to the church on the cliff top, a little to the west of the camp. The noise was frightful and I wondered whether the building in ferro-concrete would take it. At 07.55 hours, just as I had helped the Bishop on with his robes, there was a terrible crash and the roof was lifted right off the building. The M.T. had gone and I had to walk the old man all the way back to the mess. The rain and wind were so strong that they took his breath away. Holding on to him grimly I eventually got to the door. My batman was in the hall.

"'For God's sake,' I cried, 'bring the old Bish a cup of tea and put some brandy in it – I think he's had it!' Unfortunately the poor old man lying back in an armchair heard every word I said, and told his audience the following summer at his old school, Eton, when he was the Speaker at their prize-giving.

"Recounting this episode, the Bishop said: 'I was only half-conscious when the chaplain got me to the mess but I can remember hearing him shout to the batman, "For Heaven's sake put some whisky in the old man's tea".' Not exactly what I said . . ."

—••⚡❌⚡••—

In one of the Japanese camps there was no bishop and few laughs, but there Methodist padre Christopher Ross ran his "Free church faculty".

"Here", he later wrote, "I trained fifty men who would be able to conduct simple services if ever they were in a camp without a padre. I'll never know how many souls had Christian burial and Christian comfort in lonely jungle railway camps through the ministries of my lay preachers . . ."

Father Pat Rorke, remembering back to his P.O.W. camps in Java and Sumatra, says, "It was a strange experience preparing for death men of every denomination and none – Dutch, British, mixed race, even a son of the prophet. There were devout Catholics to whom I gave Extreme Unction and 'old sweats' who called themselves 'C. of E.' and had probably never said a prayer in their lives – some did not know the Lord's Prayer. There were devoted Protestants, easy to talk to. To the Mahommedan I spoke of the goodness and love of God and of His care for us all; he was happy and died full of hope. Every one of those, except those who died unexpectedly, died with at least some prayer said. This continued to the end. Sadly the men went on dying even after we were free, till the Dakotas came and took them away . . ."

The duty of burying young men in what should have been their prime fell heavily on the padres, sometimes having to conduct mass funerals.

One padre, of independent views, found difficulties with the Anglican funeral service. "How could you say", he insists, "'Forasmuch as it hath pleased Almighty God to take unto Himself the soul of our dear brother here departed?' It did violence to your feelings . . . How could you pray, 'Suffer us not at our last hour through any pains of death to fall from Thee?' I used to substitute Newman's lovely prayer 'O Lord support us . . .' and the Irish Church's prayer for the bereaved. And I always had a prayer for the departed. For the Lesson I read an extract from Revelation 21 and we said the Twenty-third Psalm. The Last Post has always appealed to me and I think it is the most suitable note on which to conclude a service funeral . . ."

In Belgium, in the winter of 1944–45, at the Brussels cemetery, this padre took the funeral of a Salvation Army woman soldier who had been killed by a flying bomb. "I said I would be honoured. At the committal, as soon as I got to the words 'dust to dust' the whole considerable company burst into 'Hallelujah!' Our sister is promoted to Glory! Said I, writing to my wife, 'A real Christian burial – no gloom, no mourning; God had wiped away the tears from their eyes.'"

Many theological problems and personal quandaries were wrestled with in Padres' Hours and Moral Leadership courses, when the padres had great opportunities but also challenges. As William Hopkins says, "Our main problem was reconciling a belief in a God of Love with the horror of modern warfare . . ."

For some of the servicemen, expeditions to sites of holy repute were impressive, and some padres took every opportunity to pass on the Christian message in this way. Bill Story recalls, "I took several parties on sight-seeing tours of the sacred sites. I tried it with Indian troops but found I could not do 'American-style' quick visits with them. In churches they promptly knelt on their bare knees on the stone floors in the aisle. I was reminded of the tremendous part played by prayer and meditation in their religion. These visits seemed valuable to the men . . . we spent nine months in and around the Holy Land and it was a great joy . . ."

7

The Response

The famous World War I padre "Woodbine Willie" said, of purely "spiritual works" – "It is all muddled and mixed. Take a box of fags in your haversack and a great deal of love in your heart and go up to them; laugh with them, joke with them. You can pray *with* them sometimes, but pray *for* them always." This word struck home to the most highly-decorated of all the World War I chaplains, the Rev. Theo Hardy, V.C., who went humbly to learn of "Woodbine Willie" and remembered his quip and quoted it before he died.

This attitude prevailed also in World War II. The padres did their utmost, in static situations and in the heat of battle, to inspire a spiritual awareness and to offer Christian resources, but no one can easily discern the response of human hearts. Living padres and those who have left us make quite a few points on this topic. The basic situation is plainly put by one chaplain who said: "Servicemen are a majority without deep reflection. They are indeed serving, neither good nor bad, but as other men."

Dermot Quinlan, speaking of compulsory parade services, says "On the whole, the men responded cheerfully. Holy Communion was always voluntary. Sometimes the response was encouraging. Once I had seventeen communicants out of one hundred men, midweek. This was my birthday – a bonus. On active service, I prepared thirty-nine men and ten women for Confirmation."

Young padres had at first much to learn. Harry Lannigan tells of the first sermon he preached on church parade, which he felt had not proved too much of an ordeal. This had a sequel six months later in Africa, when a Sergeant asked him: "Padre, do you remember the first sermon you preached?" "Indeed I do." "Well," said the Sergeant, "I said to my mate, 'That would have been a bloody good sermon if only I had known what he was talking about.'" "This," says Harry, "I think was the finest lesson in homiletics I ever had. We play around with words in the pulpit to an audience who perhaps over the years has acquired some inkling of the meaning of our jargon, and we forget that 'the man outside' has never learned even the alphabet of the pulpit."

He went on to say: "In quiet periods later I had plenty of time and opportunity to hold services and meet men in small groups. These were both stimulating and depressing. They displayed a tremendous ignorance of what the Christian faith was and an arrogance about their lack of knowledge. It usually took the line 'You believe this and no intelligent man could believe it'. Often it was impossible to let the questioner see that we did *not* believe what he said we did. Side by side there was, of course, the individual of any rank who could be genuinely seeking faith to hold on to."

Patrick Rorke, in his Far Eastern P.O.W. camp, preached to all and sundry on Sundays. "Sometimes lads came because they felt, perhaps only half-consciously, the need of God; they knew that the priest and they were sharing exactly the same hardships. He had the same hopes and lived by the same patience as they did. He was one of themselves in every way, clad in similar rags and dirty bandages, equally liable to be beaten by an unpleasant guard, and grubbing for food as they did. Still, he was the priest, and they squatted round on the grass to listen . . . I shall never be able to preach like that again . . ."

Arthur Jestice puts forward the point that "When men live in daily uncertainty of life they are particularly open". This is echoed by Murray Raw who remembers "Going out, on troopship, church services were packed. On the way home in 1945 – a mere handful. Danger had gone!"

Different forms of service life brought different problems to be faced. William Hopkins speaks about the famous "Few" airmen, and remembers the days following the Battle of Britain. "These young men came and talked to us; our talks of course were of a private nature. Many were decent-living, healthy-minded pagans, for whom Christian fellowship seemed to have little appeal. Yet there was often a real awareness of the things of the Spirit. Among these young men who faced danger daily, one said he had never before thought much about God until those few months. 'You seem to get sort of near to things up there', he said."

Robert Clements recalls, "Particularly in the mid years of the war one met many deeply religious airmen eager to co-operate. In the Fighter Force, some C.O.s were very co-operative; a very few were afraid that religion would 'make pilots morbid or think too much'. Anyway, a caring chaplain was a tangible reminder that God cares."

In a rather different situation were the W.A.A.F. in the care of H.M. Connop-Price at RAF Chicksands. "This was a Y station monitoring enemy broadcasts. Three shifts, three hundred and sixty-five days a year. All messages were in code, so the operators could in no way relate their war work to the progress of the war. This impersonality became too much for some of them, and I found myself working closely with the M.O.s and W.A.A.F. Officers in caring for those under stress. Problems were accentuated because the work was secret and they all had to be screened."

The influence of the padres on personnel was sometimes surprising and seemingly irrational. A tall thin airman went one day to speak to his chaplain. "I'm a communist", he began. "Good bloody-oh", replied the padre. Their conversation was brief. About twenty years later, the padre now relates, there was a knock at his door and there stood the tall thin former airman. "How good to see you", greeted the padre. "Fancy you remembering me", said the young man. He went on to tell how he had become a churchwarden in his church at home, and wanted his former padre to know about this. "Do you know why I became a churchman?" he asked. "It was because when I told you I was a communist, you just said 'good bloody-oh . . .'"

Another padre was a catalyst. David Izzett, whose main emphasis was "be accessible", takes us back to a Sunday night service in a nissen hut in the canal zone in Fayid. It was not comfortable; there was a stone floor and the chairs were very rickety. But the church was full and the padre, preaching upon the theme of "the Cross", felt that the congregation was gripped. At the back, a man came in late and grabbed a chair. He moved slightly and his chair collapsed. He put out his arms to save himself and dislodged the first rifle stacked at the back against the wall. A domino effect followed – one rifle after another crashing to the ground on the stone floor. No one turned round. The man who had brought this about came round afterwards to apologize. "Apparently", says David, "he was impressed by the way I accepted his apology, and he began to come regularly to the services and to join in our fellowship."

Herbert Davies, in his Far Eastern P.O.W. camp, says very positively that he was conscious of "a presence" there which upheld him throughout the bad times. He speaks of a Regimental Sergeant Major to whom he talked just before the war reached them both in Hong Kong. The R.S.M. had then asked, "Do you really believe all that stuff you spout on Sundays?" "Yes, of course, or else I wouldn't be here." "I can't accept all that – I think it's for women and kids."

The R.S.M. was later sent off to Japan. Herbert continues: "When we were collected all together in the Philippines at the end of the war, I ran into him in the canteen. We had a beer together and a chat. I reminded him of our much earlier conversation about belief in God, and I asked him if he was still of the same mind. 'Padre,' he replied, 'no man could go through the things I've survived and not believe in God.'"

Much good work was carried out on Moral Leadership courses and Padres' Hours. And many practical projects were set up, such as Wesley Houses. These sometimes produced their own response. Servicemen and women who met in Wesley House, Jerusalem, took part in Sunday rambles. They came across a home for blind girls in the Bethlehem area, whose U.K. support had dried up through wartime circumstances. The Wesley House people "adopted" this home and organized not only NAAFI collections but a weekly envelope system that kept the place going.

——•‡ ✕ ‡•——

The padres' response to death needed sensitive handling. They themselves were deeply challenged here. Gordon Brigg believes "It was a privilege to write to the families at home when their dear ones had been killed." It was also an immediate task to keep up the men's morale following the deaths of so many of their colleagues.

A moving story comes from Gerald O'Connell Fitz-Gerald, who says now that it was "the biggest experience of my eighty-one years". It relates to the time he spent in Macassar as the only British naval padre to be imprisoned by the Japanese. It is the story of "Clem", a member of the only party of Royal Navy survivors to be brought to Fitz-Gerald at his camp. The men were from *H.M.S. Stronghold*.

"The doctor said I must meet a Chief E.R.A. (Engine-room Artificer) who was, he thought, probably the most intelligent and best-educated of the English P.O.W.s. But this man was a convinced and instructed Marxist. I did meet him. We did not argue but it was like two people of different languages. I did not see him again for about three years. Then the doctor said, 'You must speak to your man Clem, for he knows he is going to die and he is an atheist and very unhappy and taking it out on the Sick Bay attendants, who are really mild malaria patients.' So I went to see Clem and repeated what the doctor had said. No progress! But I went to say good morning to him each day. Soon after he asked, 'Do you do crosswords?' 'Oh yes,' I said, with irony, 'but the *Times* is so late in arriving!' 'Would it amuse you to do one if I made it up?' he asked. Of course it would. I thought it might cheer him up, having something to do. He had time, alas, for only three or four.

"One day he surprised me by saying, 'Talk to me about mysticism'. I said I didn't know much about it. He said, 'If you asked me to explain the workings of a torpedo tube, though it's very dull, I could do it – it's my job. Mysticism is surely yours!' I felt rather at a loss – mysticism is a big subject. But trusting to the Good Lord I plunged into *The Cloud of Unknowing* and the Holy Ignorance of Contemplation. He made no comment.

"Soon he got much worse and was obviously dying. He lay on his bed turned away from the chair. The bed had not been moved for three days. He had dysentery. I said, 'Try to rest a bit, Clem.' 'No, I won't.' I tried again. Then he said, 'Very well, I will rest and perhaps go to sleep if you will promise to do exactly as I ask you.' Of course. So he went on. 'You will say to yourself the Lord's Prayer over and over again. I have not stopped for three or four hours and shall not stop to the end.' I bent over him and quietly kissed him. I said the most utterly stupid thing – 'Happy,

Clem, happy?' He looked radiant. 'Happy' – he said –
'I've never been really happy till now . . .'"

—·•✕•·—

A former Principal Chaplain of the Royal Air Force, A.
W. Hopkins, remembers the influence of a young
Flight Lieutenant, particularly upon his nearest and
dearest, and feels able to pass this story on.

"No one knew why the single-seater jet fighter
crashed on an ordinary routine flight. The pilot was
one of the most experienced on the Squadron, a man
of character and integrity, doubly decorated for wartime valour. The funeral the day previously had much
affected his chaplain because the man had been his
friend. The chaplain paused at the gate of the married
quarters, wondering what he should say to the dead
pilot's wife – knowing that the classic consolations in
bereavement might not do. She had given an impression of brittle superficiality, seeming to smile at her
husband's churchgoing and seriousness. Yesterday,
dry-eyed and calm, she had appeared detached from
what was taking place. When the funeral had finished,
she had said to the station padre, 'Please come and see
me tomorrow.' He wondered why.

"She began to talk at once. 'You've never thought
much of me, padre, have you? You thought I wasn't
good enough for my husband – no, let me go on. You
were right, except that you didn't know everything.
You knew my husband was truly religious and you
were sorry because I was not. What you didn't know
was that I had watched him living out his Christian
faith in the closeness of our married life, and that two

nights before he crashed, he completed the process of bringing me into the same faith. I had resisted it for so long. I got angry. I thought he was putting his God before me. But all the time I wanted that spiritual calm and serenity which he had – and now I have it too. Last Wednesday night we talked almost to morning and he prayed with me. And the light came.'

"'You see', her eyes clouded with tears for a moment and then she went on, 'I am quite quite sure now. It was tested out yesterday. I am a Christian woman now, padre. Had it not been for last Wednesday I think I might have killed myself. Now I have his faith and I know everything will be all right.'

"There is nothing to add to this, except to say that the light went on shining."

—••‡ ✗ ‡•••—

Many padres felt that prayers were continually being answered. Patrick Rorke speaks of such an occurrence in Java. "There was a definite answer to united prayer in the camp", he declares.

"A sick young American was known to be in the city hospital, a Catholic. I should visit him. But it was not permitted for me to visit hospitals outside the camp. Only when a man died. The Dutch liaison officer said there was no hope of getting permission. Also, I had only enough altar wine for about two more Masses and was unlikely to get more. I asked all the Catholics to come to Communion and to pray for these two intentions. They came in large numbers.

"The next day, when I returned to my bed space, behold, on my bed, a bottle of altar wine and a tin of hosts! And the following morning at ten, I was suddenly called and told there was a funeral party going to the outside hospital to collect a body and I could go with them. I knew that I could then make my way to the sick man and be picked up by the lorry to return. And so it was done and the American boy died fortified with the Sacraments. The Japanese Commandant never knew I had been out of the camp. So the next Sunday I offered Mass in thanksgiving and the number of communicants was again large . . ."

And a short extract from another Far Eastern P.O.W. memoir reveals that one army padre believed that in those difficult and unpropitious circumstances he had done his best to be faithful and God had used him.

Christopher Ross wrote: "At the end of the war I looked back to my ministry in the camps and I said to myself: two hundred and fifty thousand individual Holy Communions given; hundreds instructed in the faith, and over three hundred men received into membership of the Christian Church. Sick and troubled and dying ministered to. This was my 'Japanese Prison Circuit'. I was able to do the real job for which I had been ordained."

Even in Russia there was a witness to the Gospel. The tale of an amazing Good Friday service comes from Peter Gillingham, for several years a destroyer chaplain. He first relates the circumstances of some light-hearted inter-ship sports on the ice-bound quay at Polyarnoe, the naval port for Murmansk, where his destroyer flotilla was awaiting the return convoy. He noticed money changing hands but says the event was a great success. Amusingly, the Russians seemed to have the idea that the sack and three-legged race participants were men under punishment, flogged the length of the quay between hundreds of shouting seamen, who, when their man fell over on the ice, rushed forward, dragged him to his feet and with an encouraging kick up the backside, set him on his way.

The date was Thursday 6th April 1944. Having a drink with Captain McCoy, the padre expressed his disappointment at not having a service to mark Good Friday. "Give me half an hour," said the Captain, "and we'll surprise God and the Russians too." Soon, "Flags" was summoned and told to signal all ships. Every available seaman was to attend church service in the Red Navy club at 10 A.M. on Good Friday.

Next day, hundreds of British seamen trudged through the snow to this impressive building, where a service was held.

Says Peter today, "The British sailor is not outwardly a religious animal but he has a heart that beats. So he knew he was in atheist Russia and some deep instinct responded. We sang 'There is a green hill far away' and 'When I survey the wondrous Cross'. I preached and reminded them that we were in what had once been called Holy Russia and, under God, would one day be so called again.

"Afterwards we marched back, changed into sea-going clothing and fought our way through the waiting U-boats. On this occasion we got through without loss."

8

When the adrenaline ran

Padres are as prone to excitement as other men. Many knew times of fierce physical and mental reaction. When questioned about his reminiscences, Parachute padre Whitfield Foy at once said, "Outside my pastoral duties I remember most clearly being involved in airborne action".

Bill Story recalls the time when, Mersah Matruh having been held for a week, they were told to destroy all war material and move out. This they did after dark.

"Driving through the desert, I did not catch the words of the C.O. who shouted something and rushed off. We found ourselves in total blackness and silence. The Major of this outfit asked if I would drive his truck, as he had no driver, and I agreed. His instructions seemed obscure. Suddenly we found ourselves in the midst of German tank laagers and were being fired at. I 'trod on the gas' and tore down the track. Eventually the truck went over the edge of an escarpment. I crashed down, all four wheels together on the scree slope. We skidded and came to rest on a huge boulder. Amazingly, we were all intact. Two armoured cars appeared on the skyline but did not see us, and presumably hardly expected us to have survived that crash. After a long night roaring past German laagers, dawn came and we saw a British tank. Thank goodness, we could now not be far from the coast road.

"I could now relax a little. I was conscious of the stimulation mentioned in an old Zane Grey 'western' I had read, where he describes a manhunt from the viewpoint of the hunted. Fear, exhilaration, desperation, exaltation. I was conscious of these emotions to an extent never before or since experienced. My brain seemed to be acting at three or four times its normal speed, and I could hear it ticking, an insistent ticking. I have never felt this at any other time. I can pay a tribute to the old pre-war Morris pickup!"

Other incidents are recalled of "lucky escapes" or "merciful providence". One padre had gone with stretcher-bearers to collect a body. As he leaned over, somebody shouted, "Don't move, sir!" Right at his toe were the prongs of a mine . . .

John King, lying up motionless in a wood before his capture in France, felt a German soldier, chopping wood for a fire, grab hold of his heel in mistake for a tree stump and use it to haul himself up a hillock. A nasty moment, but King was not discovered at that point.

Norman Hurst was taking an informal service one Sunday afternoon in an Air Sea Rescue dispersal hut. After the service, a call came to go to the rescue of a pilot who had come down in the North Sea. "The chaps asked me if I would go with them and I said yes. I was putting on flying gear when I suddenly asked how long they thought they were likely to be. About five or six hours. 'Oh,' I said, 'then I can't come – I have another service before then.' Their plane and the crew were never seen again; they too must have come down in the sea."

David Walters does not forget the occasion when

the *Khedive Ismail*, the Commodore's ship, escorting a convoy from Mombasa to Colombo, was struck by a Japanese torpedo. It sank in little more than twenty seconds, with over a thousand lives lost. Walters, chaplain of the cruiser *Hawkins*, next in station, watched this horrific event, then saw the tracks of two more torpedos coming straight towards the *Hawkins*. "Mercifully, they were both set wrongly and one went right underneath us amidships and the other lopped along the surface and narrowly missed our bows . . ."

Memories remain. Robert Clements recalls a somewhat eerie night he spent alone in the advance to Tunisia, "A night all by myself in charge of a German field hospital at Merseh Matruh which was complete with German junior doctors and orderlies left behind with the seriously wounded when the Germans retreated."

Harry Lannigan wrote in his diary of the time he entered Randazzo, where they met no opposition but where there had been considerable bombing. As the battalion was walking over a huge pile of rubble, two companies passed over safely but as H.Q. company crossed there was a loud explosion and three men were killed and seven wounded.

"We cleared the casualties. Just then there was another explosion and I went sailing through the air and landed flat on my face. I thought 'This is it!' After a few seconds I gingerly got up and felt myself all over. I was amazed to be still alive."

One experience practically had stretcher-bearers passing out. "I was young and naïve then", wrote the padre concerned later, "but sometimes naïvety is an effective weapon."

He was approached by two German officer cadets, fully armed. "I walked swiftly towards them and they both put their hands in the air. In perhaps my innocence I said in my halting German, 'Wait a minute, boys, I am a chaplain, I have no weapons. I have no intention of trying to fight you. Do you want me to surrender to you?' To my relief, they said, 'No, we are your prisoners. We are fed up with trying to catch up with our own army.'

"I said, 'Thank you – perhaps you should give me your guns – or on second thoughts, dismantle them.' They proceeded to smash them. During this interlude, my stretcher-bearers were looking green but they did not know that worse was to follow. The battlefield was littered with rifles, grenades, ammunition, etc. I decided it was better gathered up. I told the stretcher-bearers and the Germans to gather up everything. When I told the Germans to dismantle grenades and Schmeissers, I thought my stretcher-bearers were going to faint!"

Stretched nerves were experienced by the late chaplain Darrell Bunt, when he sat waiting for events to unfold on the battleship *Duke of York*, at Christmas time 1943. The *Duke of York* was about to participate in an action later to be known as the battle of the North Cape. In the fight to protect a convoy, the *Duke of York* with other ships was shadowing the German cruiser *Scharnhorst*. After a battle of great fierceness she would eventually see the *Scharnhorst* sink beneath the icy waters of the North Cape, with most of her crew of nearly two thousand men.

Chaplain Bunt had been allotted a first-aid post sited in the recreation space in the bridge superstructure. "There was nothing then to do but to sit around and speculate; we could not but envy those in the ship who had plenty to occupy their minds. Our first-aid party consisted of day-men and a sick-bay rating. For many on board this was their first taste of action, so it was understandable that there should be a mixture of excitement and apprehension." As it happened, the *Duke of York* suffered no casualties.

Vincent Parkin tells a tale with a naval element. He had joined the 124 Wing 2nd T.A.F. and found that the Senior Medical Officer had been with him at R.A.F. Filey. They decided that when they crossed to Normandy they would share a tent — being issued with one apiece, and retain the other for storage. "We had been told to expect a third casualties, so it seemed to me that the Sick Quarters would be a good place for the chaplain. Accordingly when we reached a point between Caen and Bayeux, we dug a couple of trenches inside our sleeping tent and dropped our camp beds into these, so that when in bed we were below ground level and reasonably secure."

Parkin goes on: "During the first night we heard shells droning overhead and expected to find in the morning that the airstrip was out of action and our mess — an old chateau — destroyed. But everything looked normal in daylight, and we found that the droning shells had been from *H.M.S. Rodney*'s 15-inch guns as she fired away over us at the German positions . . . A few nights later, there was more shell fire and the doc and I lay in our beds bellowing 'Good old *Rodney*! That's the stuff!' In the morning we found smoke and flames from our airstrip – we were being shelled by German 88mm guns."

The chaplain of *H.M.S. Rodney* himself passed through stirring events. Within a few days of joining this ship, she crossed to Normandy and with her huge guns bombarded the occupied island of Alderney. Says Gordon Taylor, "I did not have to wait long to hear the guns fire in anger. I watched the whole bombardment from the (topmost) Admiral's bridge." For this service, the *Rodney* gained the Battle Honour "English channel". Later, after sailing in the Russian convoy J. W. 60 to Murmansk, the return journey was hazardous. While still in the Barents Sea, they were attacked and two merchant ships abeam were struck by torpedos fired by U.310. "It was very distressing", recalls Gordon Taylor, "to have to drive on while men were in the water. We did have, unusually, two rescue ships with us and I believe fifty-seven men were rescued from one ship and sixty-seven from the other. Planes from the carriers sank U.921 in reply. These convoys gave the *Rodney* her last Battle Honour – 'Arctic'. The picture of it all is for ever etched on my mind's eye . . ."

Tom Warner, a "flying padre", tells of the dangerous thrill of seeing the invasion forces below him. He went off on 6th June 1944 in H for Harry 180 Squadron.

"It turned out to be D-Day but we had not been told. We were to bomb a bridge at Caen but missed it. On the way back, through a hole in the clouds, I saw ships by the dozen and a tremendous wake behind them. 'It's the invasion!' I cried – 'let's go down and have a look.' 'You heard what the C.O. said – we're not to go below 3,000 feet.' To which I made a retort. Down we went but *Talybont* was below and, mistaking us for a Dornier, let us have it. We got out of the way through the clouds jolly sharpish. But we'd seen the invasion. On landing I grabbed my escape kit, dinghy and parachute and ran off to the Intelligence tent. I forgot the guy ropes and my face hit the mud. It was raining and I went to bed about four o'clock."

Action pursued Tom Warner. "Never a dull moment in the Shetlands", he says today with a grin.

Sitting in his office one evening, after handing out "comforts" e.g. knitted scarves, pullovers, etc., he heard an almighty crash. A Beaufort torpedo carrier had swung off the runway and had come up the sand dunes, coming to rest with the nose through the comfort department of the hut. The crew scrambled out, and the fire engine was there within seconds and appeared to extinguish the fire. Says Warner, "I saw the torpedo still in position under the belly. The blood wagon took the crew away and within half an hour the firemen went, leaving myself, the Signals officer and the Engineering officer to survey the desolation. My office was a write-off.

"Suddenly the aircraft burst into flames. We fought the flames with three fire-extinguishers but this was dangerous in the extreme. Soon, the torpedo, incredible as it sounds, was red hot and there we were trying to put out a blaze like that! The first thing to do was to run like hell but so long as Watson was using a fire extinguisher I was not going to be the first to run. Cowardice on my part I know ... suddenly the I/C Ops tannoyed, 'All personnel are to keep at least eight hundred yards from the burning aircraft'. I obeyed that order as never before or since, but in my mad dash from the flames, fell into a sandpit and then the plane went up – I reckon about seven or eight hundred feet – with a blast that went right over my head. I was the Senior Officer present but I could not order the two Flight Lieutenants to stop being idiots and run, because I was not permitted to give an executive order. I have no doubt now that it was my duty to tell them to get out of it, but I was afraid of being seen to be afraid. Had we all been killed – and we escaped death by seconds only – it would I think have been my fault. Aristotle would not have congratulated me on my courage when I reached Hades . . ."

Some adventures bore a cloak-and-dagger element. Former naval padre Ronald Bradwell usually teamed with Father W. E. Devine, M.C., since they had the same vast area to cover.

"Once," says Bradwell, "we were visiting the Yugoslav port of Split towards the end of hostilities. Father Devine asked me to accompany him to the house of the local Catholic priest. I was to stand outside the house and whistle loudly if I saw any character taking too much interest in the house. This I did. Then Father Devine came rushing out, in a most agitated state.

"'Come on, Bradwell, we must get back.' 'Why? What has happened?' 'I can't tell you now, Bradwell, I'll tell you after the war. I must get to Rome. I must see the Pope.' So we caught the next gun-boat returning to Ancona, and there Father Devine left me in great haste and went on his secret mission to Rome. I never did hear what it was all about, but those were the days when Cardinal Mindszenty and other Catholic prelates were in extreme danger, and I believe it was with secret information that Father Devine made his urgent journey to Rome."

In the tension of the times, some bizarre incidents were recorded. Bill Story tells a tale that was going round during the desert warfare.

"One of our units was driving in the open desert after dark. The enemy was not far behind and, judging by the firing, was on either flank too. Then this unit came to a line of barbed wire marking a minefield right across their path. They appeared to be pinned there in a hopeless position. The officers were discussing whether to risk trying to penetrate the minefield as a desperate expedient when a signaller rode up on his motor-cycle. He was well-known to the O.C. and others. He said, 'Excuse me, sir. I know this minefield. I have been through it in daylight several times. If you care to follow me, I can lead you by the only safe way through.' They agreed and he did indeed lead the whole group safely through. He then saluted and said, 'I must rejoin my unit now, sir,' and rode off. Two days later the O.C. was relating this incident to the C.S.O. and named the signaller.

"'Who did you say it was?' asked the C.S.O. 'For he was killed four days ago and I attended his funeral . . .'"

The same padre recounts another desert story, not supernatural but reminding us of the problems of strange terrain. He says, "We were in an area liable to enemy air action, so had to maintain rigorous blackout. We stopped at regular sites for one or two nights, and tents were scattered at two hundred yard intervals over a vast area. Finding your own tent at night could be a long and difficult operation. You took a bearing by day from the mess tent door to some tent or object, then another from there and so on. After dark, you left the mess and walked two hundred paces in what you hoped was the right direction with the help of the stars. If you did not stumble on object No. 1 at once, you lay down and tried to locate it against the starry sky. So you proceeded until you found your own tent, which could well be object No. 5.

"One night a junior chaplain just out from England was my guest on his way to take up a posting. He left the mess and plunged out into the abysmal dark outside. Three quarters of an hour later he staggered back into the mess and sank down exhausted, having failed to find his tent – i.e. the visitors' tent, only two hundred yards away. I offered to take him. We stood at the mess door and I took a bearing half left and we walked two hundred paces straight to his tent. He was most impressed. Next morning, I looked out from the mess and realized that this had been a complete fluke; the visitors' tent was forty-five degrees from the bearing I had thought I was taking in the dark."

—•◦•—

9

I can't see what more I did . . .

Death and Glory were not the aims of the chaplains, but some were faithful to the end and many achieved gallantry and merit that surprised them and of which they were hardly aware. A typical response was that of Bishop Ross Hook, the only chaplain in the R.N.V.R. to be given the Military Cross, which he was awarded while serving with the Commandos in Yugoslavia. When invited to comment upon his award he now says – "I've never known what I was supposed to have done more than anyone else . . ."

This attitude typifies those of men in the chaplaincy service who received awards for gallantry and meritorious conduct. Like most "heroes" they are rather embarrassed by their awards – proud of the honour conferred but often anxious to point out that they feel they represent many other people. Sometimes they simply say they did "nothing special".

It is agreed that circumstances played a part. Says Bill Story, "Padres of Other Denominations were usually posted to supporting troops (unless Scottish, when they went to a Scots fighting regiment). The C. of E. padres attached to units with a nominal seventy per cent C. of E. membership would be with the major regiments up forward and so suffered more casualties

– and had more chances of getting an M.C. All my chaplains in the 10th Indian Division earned and received the M.C. before the end of the campaign in Italy. I had no Free Church chaplains, and the R.C. chaplain was at Rear Division with me."

Nevertheless, citations make thrilling and humbling reading, and honour deserves to be paid to the chaplains who did receive awards. Basically, these stories are examples of Christian selflessness, tales of situations where the padres totally forgot themselves and remembered only their vocation as servants of the One who gave His life for the many. In most cases they survived grim circumstances; in a lesser number they were faithful to the last and gave their own lives.

The only Victoria Cross award to a chaplain in World War II went to a Canadian Presbyterian minister, the Rev. John Weir Foote, and was won at the time of the disastrous Dieppe raid of 1942. He was given the award for his "extraordinary heroism in helping Allied troops to re-embark and make good their escape to England". He spent much of the war later in a German P.O.W. camp and said, "If I did anything of value, it was ministering to the captured troops in the prison camps. The action at Dieppe was the easy part of it."

He felt that the valour of all the fighting men of his regiment had been honoured by his V.C., and handed his Cross to the regiment, the Royal Hamilton Light Infantry. But his heroism was not overlooked or forgotten by the Royal Canadian Legion, and in Grafton, Ontario, a cairn was raised in his honour, made from local stones blended with some brought back from the Dieppe beaches.

The Rev. Neville Metcalfe, army chaplain, received the Distinguished Service Order for conduct during three hectic days in the retreat from Rangoon in South Burma to Imphal in North India – March 1942. In the area of Pegu, in Southern Burma, Japanese activity was intense, and Padre Metcalfe became separated from his own regiment, the 7th Queen's Own Hussars. He joined some Cameronians and flung himself into collecting and caring for casualties. There were many burials. One of the Cameronians' M.O.s was killed, and shortly afterwards their ambulance was destroyed by a mortar shell. Metcalfe used his car as a temporary ambulance and drove the wounded back to the hospital in Pegu. Arriving there, a Japanese bomb dropped on one wing of the hospital, increasing casualties. In true British fashion, Metcalfe set up a small canteen and provided hot tea. He then heard that his regiment was pulling out of Pegu that night to try to break the Japanese road block and enable wounded to be got out. He remained with the sick and gave burial to the mounting numbers of dead. At night he was busy trying to relieve the wounded, and remembers rewinding bandages which in the intense heat became unbearably tight. Burials were carried out in batches, using as communal graves the network of slit trenches.

At first light, some Cameronians' lorries arrived and the wounded were carefully loaded into them. The convoy began its dangerous exit from Pegu. There were problems getting over the bridge across the river – which the rear party was about to blow up. Eventually the convoy rumbled on its way, and Neville joined up with a small force of Cameronians. Heavy Japanese fire compelled them to take cover under their lorries and then to retreat down the road by way of the ditches, passing the awful carnage of the road block. Metcalfe wanted to establish the identities of the pitiful human remains but was suddenly blown into a ditch. He was slightly wounded by mortar fire.

In the ensuing lull, the whole party melted into the jungle and began a trek to the village of Hlegu, hoping to rejoin the rest of the force. This was a march of about twenty-five miles.

Writing in the *Journal* of the Royal Army Chaplains' Department, Neville Metcalfe explained:

> Thanks to the Japanese desire to get to the loot of Rangoon as quickly as possible, and to the darkness of a moonless night, we were able to gain our objective without the loss of a single man.
>
> One thing I will always personally remember that journey for was the soreness of my feet . . . I had lost my shoes in the hectic rushes.

The citation for his award speaks of "Magnificent conduct throughout the Pegu operations. His courage, unfailing cheerfulness and complete disregard for his own personal safety have been an inspiration and encouragement to all Ranks."

Not only did this padre work flat out to bring comfort and spiritual resources to those in need, but his award is evidence of an appreciation of his morale-boosting cheerfulness, pressing on in his stockinged feet when those around him were footsore and weary also. He survived to become involved in many further actions, to remain a chaplain for thirty-three years and is with us still, seemingly as ebullient as ever.

Padre Metcalfe has never mentioned his award. But he has paid tribute to the way in which "soldiers of all ranks faced up to crisis, despite their sometimes inadequate backgrounds. They were a great challenge. My faith was definitely deepened by these soldiers."

The Military Cross awarded to J. Fraser McLuskey was earned in different circumstances. This lively padre volunteered for the Special Air Service of the Army, and, determined to go with the troops, was parachuted into France in June 1944. He jumped with the main body of A Squadron behind enemy lines. During the following three months he carried out his duties with courage and determination. When the area was full of German convoys and patrols, he made several long and dangerous journeys between the base and outlying patrols in a civilian car with only a driver, obtaining valuable information. The citation which gives this information concludes: "His bravery, steadiness and cheerfulness in all situations and complete disregard for personal safety served as an inspiration to the whole Squadron."

There seems to have been little excitement for another M.C. recipient – just immersion among the wounded and dead. In 1943 John Morson found his role in the Advanced Dressing Station at Brigade H.Q. during the Tunisian campaign. Hundreds of wounded were passing through this Dressing Station, and John helped with dressings and acted as stretcher-bearer, as well as giving spiritual comfort. Many times he went forward to the Regiments to men who lay dying on the battlefields, staying with them and comforting them to the end. Then he was disciplined in the sad task of identifying, burying and looking after the effects of fatal casualties, and writing to the next of kin.

The citation which describes these challenging days says, "No matter how intense the shelling or bombing he was always on the spot to carry out his duties and was a source of inspiration to all he came in contact with."

The banks of the Italian river Gari were the scene of courage and determination shown by the Rev. Ronald Edwards in May 1944, for which he received the D.S.O. Enemy mortar and machine-gun fire attempted to frustrate the gathering of wounded and dying men from the banks. As Edwards was taking away some wounded in his jeep, from the near bank, the tyres of the jeep were punctured. Next day a message stated that about forty men lay wounded on the far bank, where soldiers were pinned down by enemy machine-gun fire.

Padre Edwards volunteered to cross the river and try to bring help to the wounded men. Together with Major Downie of the R.A.M.C. and one runner, they made for the river in full view of the enemy. Ronald swam the river with a length of signal cable, by means of which he pulled Major Downie, with a supply of splints and dressings, across. The enemy opened up on the bank with machine-gun and shell fire. The runner led the two officers to the wounded men and they calmly set about rendering first-aid under fire.

Ronald then swam back to the near bank. He saw that an attempt was being made to salvage an assault boat in midstream. Still under fire, he tied a rope round his waist, went back into the water and swam out to the boat, which was then able to be used to ferry the wounded to safety.

Here again the citation speaks of "courage, outstanding devotion to duty and complete disregard for his own safety . . . but for his courageous swimming of the river, the time in which help could have reached the wounded on the far bank would have been greatly prolonged."

Some padres were less fortunate and did not survive the dangers of war. Almost one hundred army chaplains died while serving, faithful to the ideals of the Service and of their Faith.

Royal Air Force padres did not usually find themselves in quite such vulnerable positions, but when they did, their response was equally gallant. In strange circumstances, Geoffrey Clarence Harding received what he understands to be the only military decoration awarded to an R.A.F. padre – the M.C. It happened thus.

He was padre to a small R.A.F. detachment called a Base Defence Sector. At the crucial time of D-Day in June 1944, their job was to land and drive some miles inland and set up radar equipment, known as "half-cheeses", to intercept enemy fighters at night and defend the beachhead. This unit had been lent to the Americans. On 7th June they set off and landed on the beach known as Omaha. "Things had gone badly wrong", remembers Geoffrey today, "and the formidable steel and concrete defences had only been breached in one place." They waded ashore, soaked through, and found a line of American wounded who had dragged themselves above the high-water mark. "Some trucks got ashore. I found dry clothes but we were immediately under fire and our radar stuff was soon destroyed. The American medical services had been wiped out and our doctor and one orderly worked round the clock to help the wounded."

Harding hurried about doing what he could. He now says he was amazed at the rage he felt within himself that they were being shot at.

It was essential to get off that open beach, and in the evening he made a careful recce and found a house with a courtyard, though there were Germans very near by. "I started moving the wounded up to this improvised casualty station and the rest of the unit came too. Anything to get out of that shell fire! We went on doing our best for the wounded until an efficient medical unit came next morning . . ."

The relevant citation speaks of this padre's "Gallantry and disregard for his own safety" throughout this thirty-six hours of hell. Yet he himself still feels uneasy at his decoration. "At the time I could only think of the P.B.I. (infantrymen) slogging it out in the bocage country and taking their lives in their hands every day."

Another Royal Air Force padre who met disaster in an unexpected situation was Herbert Cecil Pugh. He was truly "faithful unto death" and was posthumously awarded the George Cross. Herbert embarked on *H.M.T. Anselm*, joining 1300 passengers bound for West Africa in July 1941. Alas, she was torpedoed in the Atlantic in the early hours of 5th July, when one torpedo hit a hold on C deck, destroying the normal means of escape.

Padre Pugh was seen to come on deck hurriedly, in a dressing gown, and go about giving help. He comforted the injured, helped with the boats and rafts, and went to the lower sections where men were quartered. When he heard that a number of injured airmen were trapped in the damaged hold, he insisted on being lowered into it by rope. People did not want him to go because the hold was below the water line and the decks were already awash; to go down was to go to certain death. He brushed this aside and said he must be where his men were. The deck level was already caving in and the hold was three parts full of water. When he knelt to pray, the water reached his shoulders.

Within a few minutes the ship plunged and sank, and Herbert Pugh was never seen again. He could have saved his own life but, in the best traditions of the Service and of the Christian ministry, he gave up his life for others.

A naval chaplain for whom also, in the end, the waters proved too strong, was Christopher Champain Tanner, the chaplain of the cruiser *Fiji*. In 1941, Royal Navy ships tried to prevent German seaborne landings in Crete. They inflicted heavy losses on the invasion convoy but encountered heavy air attacks. The destroyer *Greyhound* was sunk and the *Fiji* was among those ordered to assist and rescue survivors. There was continuous air attack. The *Fiji*, with almost all her anti-aircraft ammunition gone, moved away but was eventually sunk by a bomb from a single aircraft.

The chaplain, Christopher Tanner, was a Rugby international and a strong swimmer. He was among the last to leave his ship, and when she sank he used his considerable strength to save others and help men to rafts. A rescuing destroyer approached, and Tanner swam back and forth, taking disabled men or those who could not swim and conveying them to safety. He made thirty life-saving trips in this way. By now he was rapidly becoming exhausted but forced himself to make one last effort, for just one more remained to be rescued. Despite protests from onlookers, Tanner got the last man aboard and was then himself hauled on to the destroyer where he collapsed. Not long afterwards, he died. In April 1942 he was posthumously awarded the Albert Medal. He was one of sixteen naval chaplains who perished through enemy action in World War II.

—••f)(}••—

An unique award, that of the only D.S.O. to be won by a naval chaplain during the Second World War, was gazetted in June 1941 for Henry Morgan Lloyd. This was for "Great courage and devotion to duty in the face of enemy air attack".

Looking back fifty years, Henry Morgan Lloyd relates his own account of the events of the beginning of June.

"The great aircraft carrier *Illustrious* was a magnificent ship with an outstanding captain, a man of prayer. Following the famous attack on Taranto which in November 1940 devastated the Italian fleet, the following January the Axis powers took their revenge with a formidable attack by German aircraft. In a series of dive-bombing raids the *Illustrious* was hit a number of times – this wrecked the flight deck and penetrated the great hangar with dreadful effect – the ship was on fire fore and aft, and most guns put out of action – the attacks continued by night but by brilliant seamanship and superhuman effort, she made her way into the Grand Harbour at Malta and eventually returned to Alexandria to fight another day.

"One of the most difficult aspects of life in the massive carrier was that in action the vast majority of the ship's company were closed up at their action stations and could not know what was happening – even whether explosions were hits or near misses – such was the din of the battle. I was given the task of broadcasting at certain points to the ship's company, from a position on the bridge whenever action stations were called for – and woe betide the padre if he was not on the mark quickly! I was to tell everyone what was happening and give a clear, concise account, taking care not to exceed my brief. This was made possible by the new use of radar – so one could say where and what the approach threat was going to be. The Captain required that my commentary be as calm and objective as possible at all times! In the event of the ship being in serious action, I would go as soon as expedient to the correct spot to carry out the normal duties of the padre – to minister to the wounded and dying. It was in fact my ultimate task to go out from Malta with the Captain on an ocean-going tug and commit the bodies of over one hundred and twenty friends and shipmates to the waters of the Med. – a memory which leaves me with a perpetual loathing for the futility and madness of war, a view no doubt of many a serving padre, in whose memory the horror of modern warfare is mingled with heartfelt admiration for the courage of their comrades who deemed this country and the cause of freedom worth dying for.

"When I think about these things today, a little picture comes to mind and sums things up.

"I went to help the sole survivor of a gun crew – a young West Countryman. He managed to whisper, 'Is the captain still on the bridge?' 'Yes', I said. Then with great effort he managed to say – 'Don't you worry, padre – he will bring us safely home.' This was a tribute to Denis Boyd, one of England's great sea captains, but more than that, to me it was a simple but profound expression of trust in the Lord, for I knew this young man and what was deep within his heart. Then he died beside his gun, his duty done."

—••┋❭❨❬••—

These are just a few of the chaplains of all Services who did not fail when the harsh tests came. Yet it is encouraging to know that, in spite of their daunting achievements, they were "only human".

John Charles Wallis, R.N.V.R., chaplain to the 41 (R.M.) Commando, was making his way back to the sick bay from a hill near Salerno where he had been burying the dead. He was alone, and discerned a narrowing of the track where the valley took a sharp bend and where the enemy was directing fairly accurate fire. The shadows were lengthening and there was some distance to go. Should he stay on the hillside for the night? He decided to risk it and walk on through the dangerous valley.

He now admits, "I was very frightened. On many occasions since then when using the twenty-third psalm at worship, or weddings or funerals, the words 'Though I walk thro' the valley of the shadow of death' have momentarily brought me back to that experience at Salerno . . ."

But this is the man who was awarded the D.S.C. for "Great courage and fortitude in tending the wounded and bringing in casualties during operations at Salerno in 1944 . . ."

10

Feelings

What of the chaplains themselves? What of their thoughts and feelings? In many ways these were identical to those of the servicemen and women – loneliness, fear, worry. Says Ronald Bradwell, "I found I was exactly the same as the men, lonely because of separation from my newly-wed wife." Padre Walters, of the cruiser *Hawkins*, present among the bombardment ships on the assault on Normandy in June 1944, returned to Portsmouth for re-ammunitioning. He took the opportunity to get married, but after one night's honeymoon had to go back with his ship to the beaches, leaving his wife crying on a park bench. Many of the younger padres left behind pregnant wives and tiny children – children who would scarcely know their father when he returned.

There was a bleakness for some through lack of the supportive church life to which they had been accustomed. William Hopkins comments: "Broadly speaking, a civilian minister moves among a circle of Christians and his social circle usually shares his views and principles. A chaplain may find himself living in an environment which differs widely from his own tradition, ethos and habit. Of course this gives him the opportunity to live the Faith before people who are often hungry for the eternal truths we preach."

Today, former padres speak freely about their handling of fear, experienced in dangerous situations. They agree that fear shared is much more manageable and that getting totally occupied was the best way of overcoming it. "Action and care for others casts fear out for yourself." One admits to "being scared stiff" but found he could overcome it. One remembers "It was like a physical pressure on every inch of your skin, it isolated you, especially if you were in the pitch dark waiting for something to happen."

A former army padre of many years in the chaplaincy service agrees that "bombs dropping near were frightening" but says, "I committed myself into God's hands and this gave tranquillity". Another says, "I was very much afraid one night, near the Japanese positions, and was unable to sleep. But I prayed and committed my family to God's care. Then came sleep and this was my experience ever after."

A "flying padre", who had enlisted as an R.A.F. combatant, recalls the different rituals of the men to ward off fear and, as they saw it, "bad luck". These included a four-leaf clover, the theme from William Tell played on a piccolo, and the sight of the padre himself in the plane. Speaking personally, this padre says, "In those days of action and danger, I was very conscious of being in the great hand of God. Whilst waiting there at the end of the runway, I always said to myself *'In tuas manus commendo meum spiritum'* – and that was that. One and a half minutes before taking off time, I always chewed gum which helped me to await the flak that came up thick and fast from the gunners down below."

Hywel Evans, in the long pursuit of the armoured

cruiser *Scharnhorst*, says, "Partly to quieten my own nerves I got the galley to make up some bully-beef sandwiches to take around the dinner-less sailors and waited to see where I might be needed."

Until they had been in action, many padres felt unsure of how they would cope. This seems to have worried them more than the thought of the enemy. Geoffrey Harding, remembering Omaha Beach on D-Day, writes: "Before we went I felt frightened – not, curiously enough, of being killed or wounded, but of my nerve failing at the crucial moment and of letting down myself, my unit and my profession. In the end it worked rather like stage fright."

Padres talk of states veering between "very frantic" and "doing nothing". Apart from the hanging about due to cancellation of orders, few speak of boredom, though some found they needed more action and possibly excitement. Some did something about this. Raymond Bowers was first posted to the Army School of Hygiene and Tropical Medicine, became bored and volunteered for Airborne. He then arrived at a Glider Pilot Regiment but discovered there was for him little likelihood of action there. "I made a fuss", he says "and eventually got to parachute training at Hardwick Hall . . . this was very tough but superb."

Harry Lannigan fought to get into the infantry. "A chaplain who told me he was forty-two, spent the night with us on the way to join the 5th Northamptons in the 11th Infantry Brigade. Several times I had spoken to the Senior Chaplain about a move to Infantry but nothing had come of it. It now became imperative, I thought. How could an 'old man' of forty-two be sent to Infantry when I, at that time only twenty-six, young, fit, unmarried, was well down the line? This time my plea was heard. Posting came through and though opposed by the Colonel and the Brigadier, I fought on and the posting was confirmed.

"It made a great difference to my own morale to be wearing the Battleaxe sign declaring me to be a member of the distinguished 68th. Identification with a unit or formation plays a large part in the morale of soldiers."

A few padres felt sufficiently unsettled to remuster, which Ronald Goulding did, taking his wings in the R.A.F. and becoming a Flying Officer. He now says, "I seemed to have as many opportunities of Christian service and witness as before, even to being asked to preach the sermon on V-Day celebrations by the A.O.C."

Sometimes the padres were in the "dog-house" like anybody else. An elderly former naval chaplain recalls, "The Dean sat inadvertently on my Secret List and it stuck to his coat. It was found outside and I was court-martialled for leaving 'Most Secret' in the street!" And one of the flying padres admits to being grounded for a while for some peccadillo.

When the fortunes of war took a poor turn for Britain or the war seemed to be dragging on, depression set in. Harry Lannigan tells in his memoirs how he found himself on the way back from Blida in the back of a 15 cwt truck. It was very hot and the dust was thick. "I was nearly choking. What was it all about? Depression rested heavily on me. Then suddenly everything changed. I could not explain it until I happened to notice the time and knew that, at that moment, my parents and family were having family prayers. This was perhaps the first time in my life, certainly the most vivid, when I felt the power of prayer in such a manner . . ."

Another padre acknowledges "Probably the clearest spiritual experience I have ever been granted". Bill Story tells how he got a signal about his father's illness and went on leave urgently to see him. By truck to Arras, he had hours to wait for his train and went into the great Cathedral and knelt down to pray for his father. At once there came a feeling of absolute certainty as though the father was there in person to reassure him. "I knew I would not see him alive but that did not matter now." When he reached his home, he found that his father had been buried the previous day.

Sometimes padres were almost crushed by the tragedies of the time. Jamie Mack tells how, towards the end of the war, the 6th Airborne was transported miles behind German lines round a small German village called Hamminkeln. "When the Infantry had gone through, over the bridges we had taken and held intact for them, I walked round the village and found a little Lutheran church. In the neat little churchyard I found three plots of military graves of German soldiers – 1870, when Bismarck was Chancellor, the second 1914 to 1919, and the third, new graves, 1939 onwards.

"O, God," I thought, "three generations in seventy years – when is it going to stop?"

Chaplains were not exempt from strain. Hywel Evans, then a young destroyer chaplain in the Royal Navy, remembers first the problems of the sailors.

"Sheer physical exhaustion and nervous strain. Tensions of hope and fear. Some would blow their top, others were glad of a more restrained confidant in the chaplain's cabin and would come in and just sit for a while — escaping from people. The journey to and from Russia meant three weeks in a ship about two hundred and thirty feet long for approximately two hundred and thirty men — and that space included all the deck fittings for action. And the Soviets allowed no one off the ship for exercise on the jetty alongside when we arrived, until June 1944.

"We chaplains had our strains too. Though we had our Rock, our Beacon Light, we too worried about our own families. My parents had a near miss in the fire bombing of Swansea . . . several brothers were in grim circumstances in the Services . . . the winter of 1943—44 was our darkest in the North."

Occasionally, utter revulsion overcame one. Harry Lannigan describes in his memoirs a scene after the second battle for Cassino.

Some experiences hardly bear description. Yet they happened. A badly decomposed torso was lying on a steep slope. It was not possible to do anything by way of burial except by getting below the torso and building up boulders on top of it. Whilst trying to do this I slipped and fell with a squelch right on top of it. I was violently sick. To make matters worse, we were allowed at that time only enough water for washing in the morning. All other water was for cooking. This meant that after handling corpses, like the one just mentioned, I was unable to wash my hands.

While eating my supper sandwiches, I suddenly
became aware of this and felt sick again . . .

Yet, while it is certainly true that some nightmares
have remained for fifty years, many would agree with
Ross Hook when he says, "Now I find the good things
clearer than the horrors".

Compassion was an emotion common to padres of
all services. Hywel Evans, on the *Musketeer*, afterwards
put into words his feelings as he stood on deck in the
pitch darkness of a December Arctic afternoon and
watched the German battle-cruiser *Scharnhorst*
burning.

"It was a fearsome sight. I stood on deck and
watched and prayed . . . for them, their widows and
children, and for forgiveness for mankind's inhuman-
ity which made these things necessary . . ."

A similar emotion seized William Hopkins, when he
was Assistant Principal Chaplain R.A.F. in the South-
East Asia Command; his "area" stretched from India
down to Australia. He visited Hiroshima a few months
after the bomb had been dropped. "It was a shocking
experience", he now says. "I talked and worshipped
with some survivors who were doomed to die eventually and saw the visible effects of radiation on their
faces and bodies." This experience affected him pro-
foundly. He has been looking through some words he
wrote in 1946.

"I climbed the shell of one of the few concrete
buildings which stood up to the blast and looked out
over a sea of desolation. Everything was rubble, and
here and there among it I saw the charred remains of
household effects – vases which intense heat had

melted to weird shapes, a bicycle twisted into an unrecognizable mass, a picture frame . . ."

Self-discovery, not always agreeable, was the experience of many padres. Some had to combat increasingly disturbing tendencies as the war went on. One, common to Prisoners-of-War, was a secretive hoarding of food. Also, as one confesses, "When we were twenty-five miles from Matruh, we realized it was being bombed. We said, 'Poor old Matruh is getting it tonight . . . ha ha!' A sort of selfish relief that we were not ourselves 'getting it' took over. I had noticed a similar feeling when seeing Plymouth bombed on a previous occasion." These were understandable but unwelcome reactions.

Brutalizing events naturally distressed the chaplains. Bill Story tells of a moment, in the Italian campaign, when the men encountered SS units and did not like their practices. A word went round the Indian regiment – no more prisoners – shoot to kill. "So, one more bit of humanity went out of the window . . ."

Even more distressing was an incident recorded by a youthful chaplain when he received word, in Sicily, that a young German officer had been wounded, and he was asked to go and pick the man up. When he found him, the young German was lying dead with a British bayonet in his back.

"I was stunned", wrote this padre. "I could not believe that any British soldier could do this. I tried to suspend belief but the evidence was there. The German had a letter in his pocket from his brother on the Russian front, in which I was able to read 'You should be thankful that you are in Italy. I have had my bellyful of the Russian front.' This was the last straw. Tears filled my eyes and I cried from the depths of my being – 'God, if you are a God of love, why do you allow this to happen?' Immediately there came the answer clear and straight – 'Because I am a God of Love, why do *you* allow it to happen?' It was not exactly a voice or a mystical experience, but it was real and powerful . . ."

——◆**⟨✕⟩**◆——

Mercifully, all was not gloom and doom. Most of the padres were youthful enough to get caught up in excitement and movement. One who was later killed at Salerno wrote, "How grand it is to be young! I do get a kick out of all the change and movement."

Most found relief and pleasure in simple things like hard physical exercise, sport, getting a letter from home, listening to records, and reading in some quiet corner, often difficult to secure. Herbert Davies, in his P.O.W. camp in Hong Kong, wrote in his diary a precise list of the books he read. These included *Hamlet*, the *Golden Treasury*, *Jane Eyre*, *Vanity Fair*, *The Good Companions*, *David Copperfield* and *The Keys of the Kingdom*. Card games passed many weary hours, and many padres became extraordinarily good bridge players.

Water figures in diaries and memoranda almost as often as food. Someone wrote, just prior to the retreat to Alamein, "A sea bathe was a wonderful thing. We were allowed one gallon a day of water, Officer or private soldier. Some was taken for cooking, some for drinking, leaving about a cupful for daily ablutions.

You brushed your teeth first, then washed as much of you as the water would reach. Each day you brushed off great crusts of white salt from face and knees, resulting from the drying of perspiration."

The companionship of service life was, to many, the greatest boon. Henry Babb says, "I enjoyed the life because of the excellent comradeship – and, in the P.O.W. camps, the 'Fepow spirit' (Far Eastern Prisoners of War). This Fepow spirit was really something, I can tell you!"

Most padres speak warmly of the camaraderie of those wartime days and tell of friendships made which endured for fifty years. These friendships crossed social divides. One padre searched for and found the unit of a man whose body he had identified and buried. Introducing himself to the Major, he gave the news. "Not – he's my batman. Been my best friend and servant for fourteen years." Tears streamed down the Major's face.

Memories are sometimes affectionately silly. One recalls a time "A friend and I drove wildly into Cairo in a car without brakes. We went to buy perfume for our wives and spent a hilarious hour having our forearms daubed with scent by a couple of charming houris." Another enjoyed a boisterous interlude – "When the 51st Highland Division sets out to celebrate Hogmanay and can give its mind to it, then something happens . . . they did dance well – reels and sword dances, and big dances for everybody . . ."

Travel could sometimes lift the spirits, and some padres, with an eye for beauty and for detail, made quick effective entries in their diaries, revealing a genuine spirit of place. David Izzett bought a diary in

Colombo, Ceylon, and went for jungle training. He wrote observantly of "The scorched undergrowth, contrasting green trees, some very bright. No other colours except rare red or other flowering trees. Glimpses of bright blue sky. Atmosphere very hot and dry – the wind only in the treetops. In an open truck, it was refreshing and occasionally a gorgeous delicate fragrance wafted on the hot dry air. At night, many stars glimpsed . . ."

Less peaceful was a stormy night in the jungle. Then it was a case of "Rain in sheets . . . broken tree stumps . . . lightning vivid and terrific cracks of thunder . . . trucks bogged down . . . crashing trees . . . wild vines and creepers tearing at the branches . . . a tangle of thorns and brambles – two snakes killed. Green and yellow centipedes with red legs, three-inch millipedes, black ants, ticks . . ."

In India, in Trichinopoly, it was "Sand, sand and sea. Dunes and tufts, the grass tough and patchy, with isolated palms . . . more palms and tamarinds . . . level as far as the eye can see." Later it was "everything green . . . Shining water . . . the monsoon has come."

—••€ ✖ ३••—

Padres have been asked whether they felt the wartime experience made a difference to them. Most replied "yes", that they had learned much, particularly about human relationships and quite a bit of self-discovery. Their answers are well summed up by Father Pat Rorke, now into his eighties. "I grew up", he says simply.

Some advanced in ecumenical attitudes. "In some

ways the Church was more ecumenical than the Forces", says one. And many feel that they developed in authority and in self-confidence. After a year or two, they found their way round and were more able to make independent judgements.

This sometimes involved taking a stand on principles. The diary of one padre relates how he had gone with his Commanding Officer to look for the Brigadier, who was eventually run to ground in a local brothel. The madam indicated that he was "upstairs". "As this place is out of bounds", murmured the C.O. to the padre, "I think we had better get you out of here."

"Next day I was due to take a service at Brigade H.Q. When I went to arrange this, the Brigadier said he would read the lesson. He got rather a shock when I said, 'Oh, I don't think you will — I happen to know where you were last night'. The other officers present were silent, until the Brigadier burst out laughing and congratulated me."

Tom Warner, a dynamic Irishman, and one of the R.A.F. flying padres, found himself in a caring quandary. He relates this story as follows.

"Shortly after the Duke of Kent was killed near the Moray Firth a man's body was seen dangling from a parachute that got caught on the cliffs of Fitful Head, nearly a thousand feet high, to the North-west of our camp. Apparently, a Halifax trying to make an emergency landing at Sumburgh came down-wind too low in the dark and hit the Head at about eighty feet from the top. Of course there was an explosion and this poor chap was blown out of the fuselage and his parachute opened. It was caught by a projecting rock one hundred and sixty feet over the water.

"Fitful Head is difficult to descend because the first seven hundred feet is shale and therefore mighty dangerous. Air Ministry forbade the Group Captain to attempt to rescue the body. The trouble was the cliff tends to slant inwards at about two hundred feet over the sea. I volunteered to go down provided the necessary safeguards were laid on. The negative response could not have been more forcibly expressed. It was an Air Ministry order and that was that.

"However, the body continued to dangle in the winds and gales and everyone was embarrassed. I heard an airman say – 'If it was the Duke of Kent they'd bring him up'. So I decided I'd go down myself and at least cut the cord. I approached a crofter and asked him – if I supplied a rope, would he go down the shale with me? I wouldn't ask him to go further. Willie agreed, and the day came when I went off with my driver, L. A. C. Finney, and a friend, Flight Lieutenant Taylor, to whom I confided what I was about to do and to whom I gave things for my wife. We picked up Willie and set off.

"At the top of the cliff, Finney asked me point blank if I was going down for the body. 'Yes,' I said. 'Then I'm going with you sir.' 'No, Finney, you are not – too dangerous.' 'I'm sorry, sir, but you can't stop me – I am going with you.' So down he came. Every stone that rolled down set my heart in my mouth, fearing it was Finney. But after we had 'gone over the top' and left seven hundred foot of shale behind – and Willie – I admit Finney was a great companion. The last part of the descent was the worst because we were hanging on over the sea, one hundred and sixty-five feet below us, and the cliff was slanting inwards. But luckily for us there was a huge horizontal crack in the rock that caused a protrusion about one hundred feet long and three feet wide, and it was from that crack that the body was swinging. We managed to haul it up and I took the man's tabs and we packed the body down into the crack, covering it with its parachute and stones we gathered. I said the Committal and a few more prayers, and Finney fired three shots with my revolver. Three and a half hours after we had left the top of Fitful Head we started to climb back again, and after another two hours we were on the top. Was I thankful!

"I went straight to the C.O.'s office. 'Sir,' I said, 'I have committed a court martial offence.' 'Oh, Christ', was all he said. Then I told him the story, and of course he had no alternative but to inform the Air Ministry.

"Mercifully, the Air Commodore he spoke to was appreciative and asked that I fly past the cliff, take a photo of the approximate location of the 'grave' and then go and tell the man's family about the exploit. I gave the parents a letter I had taken from the man's pocket, and they were more than grateful. In the ensuing weeks all the skin came off my hands; it had clearly taken more out of me than I cared to admit."

—••≪ ≫••—

Some chaplains maintained traditional attitudes in worship and in moral values. Others found themselves re-assessing much that they had been brought up to believe. Harry Lannigan, M.C., was one of these. In his memoirs he wrote:

> During the course of the war my theology and absolute morality suffered a complete turnover. Having been brought up to believe that sin was indivisible and that sins were easily identified, e.g. drinking, gambling, sex, etc., I soon discovered that this was too easy. Hard-drinking, sex-hunting N.C.O.s and W.O.s proved themselves so often. Many would and did give their lives for others. This was a salutary experience, teaching me the truth of the biblical saying: "The Lord does not see as man sees; men judge by appearances but the Lord judges by the heart." It was quite clear to me that there were no moral absolutes.

Large-heartedness had been noted by Father Thomas Holland, naval chaplain at the time of the Allied landings in Normandy. Many years later he recalled, "Two of us were carrying a wounded man across the open deck of an L.S.T. (which was used to evacuate the wounded) when a burst of high-fragmentation shells threw us on deck. I was greatly moved to see that my fellow worker, a burly seaman in a blue gansey, had so fallen that he completely covered our casualty with his own body. I think there you have the 'greater love' of which Our Lord spoke."

A few padres seem not to have been up to the job. An Infantry officer recalls one "scared to go out to bury the dead". He felt compassion for this man. He also remembers one who confessed to having virtually lost his faith. This padre did not feel he could withdraw and so enacted a role . . . The Officer could not ascertain any real reason other than that circumstances had totally secularized the padre. Another is remembered as "totally dedicated but became bowed beneath his load of duties and worries and thus almost incapacitated".

Asked if they consider their wartime chaplaincies well worthwhile, most respond in the affirmative. Only one asked said "not at all sure". Most felt that they were able to make good contributions, and that they came through the war better equipped for their vocation. Says one, "It was immensely worthwhile, especially from an ecumenical viewpoint and in strengthening the faith of many." And Herbert Davies says of his years in the Japanese camp, "I emerged from my experience as a P.O.W. with my spiritual life greatly enhanced. It was very worthwhile."

When hostilities ended, most temporary chaplains were demobbed and returned home. They met up with their families and renewed their vocations as priests and ministers. Some wished to forget certain incidents of the past years, some to forget almost everything. Others would continue to remember and be affected for the next fifty years. Some talk easily about events still. Some decided they enjoyed service life and remained within the chaplaincy service and went on in time into further conflicts.

I Believe
Trevor Huddleston

A simple, prayerful series of reflections on the phrases of the Creed. This is a beautiful testament of the strong, quiet inner faith of a man best known for his active role in the Church – and in the world.

The Heart of the Christian Faith
Donald Coggan

The author ". . . presents the essential core of Christianity in a marvellously simple and readable form, quite uncluttered by any excess of theological technicality."

The Yorkshire Post

Be Still and Know
Michael Ramsey

The former Archbishop of Canterbury looks at prayer in the New Testament, at what the early mystics could teach us about it, and at some practical aspects of Christian praying.

Pilgrim's Progress
John Bunyan

"A masterpiece which generation after generation of ordinary men and women have taken to their hearts."

Hugh Ross Williamson

Also available in Fount Paperbacks

A Gift for God
MOTHER TERESA OF CALCUTTA

'The force of her words is very great . . . the message is always the same, yet always fresh and striking.'

Malcolm Muggeridge

Strength to Love
MARTIN LUTHER KING

'The sermons . . . read easily and reveal a man of great purpose, humility and wisdom . . . in the turbulent context of the American race conflict, Dr King's statements have the ring of social as well as spiritual truth . . .'

Steven Kroll
The Listener

A Book of Comfort
ELIZABETH GOUDGE

'The contents are worth ten of the title: this is a careful, sensitive anthology of the illuminations in prose and verse that have prevented the world from going wholly dark over the centuries.'

Sunday Times

The Desert in the City
CARLO CARRETTO

'. . . we have been in the hands of one of the finest of modern spiritual writers, who helps us on the road of love in Christ.'

Philip Cauvin, the Universe

Also available in Fount Paperbacks

BOOKS BY C. S. LEWIS

The Abolition of Man

'It is the most perfectly reasoned defence of Natural Law
(Morality) I have ever seen, or believe to exist.'

Walter Hooper

Mere Christianity

'He has a quite unique power for making theology an attractive,
exciting and fascinating quest.'

Times Literary Supplement

God in the Dock

'This little book . . . consists of some brilliant pieces . . . This is just
the kind of book to place into the hands of an intellectual doubter
. . . It has been an unalloyed pleasure to read.'

Marcus Beverley, Christian Herald

The Great Divorce

'Mr Lewis has a rare talent for expressing spiritual truth in fresh
and striking imagery and with uncanny acumen . . . it contains
many flashes of deep insight and exposures of popular fallacies.'

Church Times

Fount Paperbacks

Fount is one of the leading paperback publishers of religious books and below are some of its recent titles.

☐ FRIENDSHIP WITH GOD David Hope   £2.95
☐ THE DARK FACE OF REALITY Martin Israel   £2.95
☐ LIVING WITH CONTRADICTION Esther de Waal   £2.95
☐ FROM EAST TO WEST Brigid Marlin   £3.95
☐ GUIDE TO THE HERE AND HEREAFTER
                         Lionel Blue/Jonathan Magonet   £4.50
☐ CHRISTIAN ENGLAND (1 Vol) David Edwards   £10.95
☐ MASTERING SADHANA Carlos Valles   £3.95
☐ THE GREAT GOD ROBBERY George Carey   £2.95
☐ CALLED TO ACTION Fran Beckett   £2.95
☐ TENSIONS Harry Williams   £2.50
☐ CONVERSION Malcolm Muggeridge   £2.95
☐ INVISIBLE NETWORK Frank Wright   £2.95
☐ THE DANCE OF LOVE Stephen Verney   £3.95
☐ THANK YOU, PADRE Joan Clifford   £2.50
☐ LIGHT AND LIFE Grazyna Sikorska   £2.95
☐ CELEBRATION Margaret Spufford   £2.95
☐ GOODNIGHT LORD Georgette Butcher   £2.95
☐ GROWING OLDER Una Kroll   £2.95

All Fount Paperbacks are available at your bookshop or newsagent, or they can be ordered by post from Fount Paperbacks, Cash Sales Department, G.P.O. Box 29, Douglas, Isle of Man. Please send purchase price plus 22p per book, maximum postage £3. Customers outside the UK send purchase price, plus 22p per book. Cheque, postal order or money order. No currency.

NAME (Block letters) _____

ADDRESS_____

_____

_____